THE COMING GOLDEN AGE

HOW TO BE KINGDOM READY

STUDY GUIDE | SIX LESSONS

DR. DAVID JEREMIAH

 Harper*Christian* Resources

The Coming Golden Age Bible Study Guide
© 2024 David P. Jeremiah
P.O. Box 3838, San Diego, CA 92163

Published in Grand Rapids, Michigan, by HarperChristian Resources. HarperChristian Resources is a registered trademark of HarperCollins Christian Publishing, Inc.

Requests for information should be sent to customercare@harpercollins.com.

ISBN 978-0-310-16796-9 (softcover)
ISBN 978-0-310-16797-6 (ebook)

Published in association with Yates & Yates, www.yates2.com.

First Printing October 2024 / Printed in the United States of America

24 25 26 27 28 LBC 5 4 3 2 1

CONTENTS

How to Use This Study Guide v

Introduction ix

LESSON 1   Thy Kingdom Come (Matthew 6:10) 1

LESSON 2   The Golden City (Jeremiah 3:17) 15

LESSON 3   King Jesus (Zechariah 14:9) 31

LESSON 4   No Devil (Revelation 20:1-3) 45

LESSON 5   Old Age in the Golden Age (Isaiah 65:20) 61

LESSON 6   The End of War (Micah 4:3) 77

Leader's Guide 93

About Dr. David Jeremiah and Turning Point 97

Stay Connected 99

HOW TO USE THIS STUDY GUIDE

The purpose of this study guide is to reinforce Dr. David Jeremiah's dynamic, in-depth teaching and to aid you in applying biblical truth to your daily life. This study guide is designed to be used in conjunction with *The Coming Golden Age* by Dr. David Jeremiah, but it may also be used by itself for personal or group study.

Structure of the Lessons

Each lesson is based on the corresponding chapter in *The Coming Golden Age* and focuses on specific passages in the Bible. Each lesson is composed of the following elements:

- **Outline:** The outline at the beginning of the lesson gives a clear, concise picture of the topic being studied and provides a helpful framework for readers as they read Dr. Jeremiah's teaching.

- **Overview:** The overview summarizes Dr. Jeremiah's teaching on the passage being studied in the lesson. You should refer to the Scripture passages in your own Bible as you study the overview. Unless otherwise indicated, Scripture verses quoted are taken from the *New King James Version*.

- **Application:** This section contains a variety of individual and group discussion questions that are designed to help you dig deeper into the lesson and the Scriptures and to apply the lesson to your daily life. For Bible study groups or Sunday school classes, these questions will provide a springboard for group discussion and interaction.

- **Did You Know?** This section presents a fascinating fact, historical note, or insight that adds a point of interest to the preceding lesson.

Personal Study

The lessons in *The Coming Golden Age Study Guide* were created to help you gain fresh insights into God's Word and develop new perspectives on topics you may have previously studied. Each lesson is designed to challenge your thinking and help you grow in your knowledge of Christ. During your study, it is our prayer that you will discover how biblical truth affects every aspect of your life and your relationship with Christ will be strengthened.

When you commit to completing this study guide, try to set apart a time, daily or weekly, to read through the lessons without distraction. Have your Bible nearby when you read the study guide so you're ready to look up verses if you need to. If you want to use a notebook to write down your thoughts, be sure to have that handy as well. Take your time to think through and answer the questions. If you plan on reading the study guide with a small group, be sure to read ahead and be prepared to take part in the weekly discussions.

Group Study

The lessons in this study guide are suitable for Sunday school classes, small-group studies, elective Bible studies, or home Bible study groups. Each person in the group should have his or her own study guide. You may wish to complete the study guide lesson as homework prior to the meeting of the group and then use the meeting time to discuss the lesson. If you are a group leader, refer to the guide at the back of this book for additional instructions on how to set up and lead your group time.

For Continuing Study

For a complete listing of Dr. Jeremiah's materials for personal and group study, call 1-800-947-1993, go online to www.DavidJeremiah.org, or write to Turning Point, P.O. Box 3838, San Diego, CA 92163.

Dr. Jeremiah's *Turning Point* program is currently heard or viewed around the world on radio, television, and the Internet in English. *Momento Decisivo*, the Spanish translation of Dr. Jeremiah's messages, can be heard on radio in Spanish-speaking countries around the world. The television broadcast is also broadcast by satellite throughout the Middle East with Arabic subtitles.

Contact Turning Point for radio and television program times and stations in your area, or visit our website at www.DavidJeremiah.org/stationlocator.

THE COMING GOLDEN AGE

INTRODUCTION

Throughout human history, our world has been steeped in war, yet human beings always seem to be searching for peace. In America, peace movements are as old as the country itself. The Quakers, a religious group that rejected violence, protested the Revolutionary War by refusing to participate in it and refusing to pay taxes that might go toward aiding violence, risking persecution from both sides.

The War of 1812 was quite a controversial war, and the Federalist party in New England opposed it for many reasons. A group of Federalists even held a convention in Connecticut where they debated (but ultimately rejected) secession from the Union.

Of course, states actually did secede from the Union later, which prompted the Civil War, and there were peace movements on both sides during that conflict. Anti-war Democrats in the North sought immediate peace. The President of the Confederacy, Jefferson Davis, had to contend with a peace movement led by his own Vice President, Alexander Stephens.[1]

One of the first public anti-war demonstrations in U.S. history happened one month after war broke out in Europe in July of 1914. On August 29, to show their opposition to American involvement in what became World War I, the Women's Peace Parade held a march down Fifth Avenue in New York City led by about 1,500 women wearing black dresses and black armbands.

Of course, the Vietnam War sparked the largest and most organized anti-war movement, including "teach-ins," "sit-ins," and other massive demonstrations that sometimes became violent. Protest songs were popular, and well-known "conscientious objectors" such as Muhammad Ali refused to report when drafted.[2]

What does all this tell us? The world longs for peace, but we can't seem to find it. Humanity has a built-in desire for peace, yet we lack the ability to find or achieve that peace on our own.

However, a day is coming when the world will know peace for a thousand years. During the Millennium, Christ will reign on earth as King. Through His power, crime will be nonexistent, wars will cease, and worshipers will fill the church pews. There will be 52,000 weeks of peace, prosperity, and universal cheer—centuries of happiness, free from war and worry. This thousand-year coming Golden Age is part of your inheritance if you're a follower of Christ.

While Christians today have Jesus as King in our hearts, there will come a time when He establishes His kingdom of glory here on earth, and life will be as it was intended before the Fall, before sin entered the world. Satan will be bound, and we will be free from his tyranny. Lifespans will be much longer, and death will be rare during this coming Golden Age. It will be like nothing we have ever experienced. It will be a precursor to our heavenly eternity with Jesus.

Though often overlooked, it's important to examine the life we will be given on the other side of the Rapture and the Tribulation. In fact, more Scripture passages address the Millennium than any other prophetic event in the Bible! And if the Rapture were to occur today, our life in the coming Golden Age would begin in just seven years.

For all these reasons and more, we can look forward to our future with Christ whenever our lives are difficult and whenever our world is filled with unrest, divisiveness, immorality, and despair.

Notes
1. "Alexander H. Stephens," *HISTORY.com*, https://www.history.com/topics/american-civil-war/alexander-h-stephens.
2. Christopher Klein, "A Timeline of U.S. Anti-War Movements," *HISTORY.com*, https://www.history.com/news/anti-war-movements-throughout-american-history.

THY KINGDOM COME

MATTHEW 6:10

In this lesson we learn about the coming thousand-year kingdom where Christ will reign perfectly over the earth.

The coming millennial kingdom of Jesus Christ on earth will be unlike any other period in human history. Though God's Word is saturated with its account, many people remain unaware of it. Because much of its description is stashed away in the books of the major and minor prophets of the Old Testament, it gets lost from view. Still, we should give the coming Golden Age considerable attention because we are potentially close to experiencing this coming kingdom ourselves.

OUTLINE

I. **The Kingdom of Grace**

II. **The Kingdom of Glory**

OVERVIEW

In the aftermath of World War I, the Red Cross recruited young American men to travel to Europe to help the suffering masses. One farm boy from Missouri caught the vision. Although he was too young to apply, he forged the date on his birth certificate and managed to join the Red Cross, eventually becoming an ambulance driver in France.

During his service there, he fell in love with the charm and elegance of French design and architecture. He took it all in—the gilded chambers of the palaces, the gardens of Versailles, the priceless paintings in the galleries of the Louvre. The whole experience was just like magic to him.

After the war, this young man returned to Europe with his wife and continued to dream of creating worlds of fantasy—of lands filled with kings and queens and castles and palaces. That young man's name was Walt Disney, and if you visit any of his eponymous theme parks today, you will see signs of royalty represented everywhere.

Walt Disney associated these fantastical and beautiful kingdoms with the highest form of happiness. C. S. Lewis theorized that our longing for these mythological worlds indicates a true desire in the human heart for a place where everything is as it should be. He believed that behind these magical myths was an ultimate reality that pulls us onward and upward.

In his book *Miracles*, Lewis defined *myth* as "at its best, a real though unfocused gleam of divine truth falling on human imagination." He continued, "The heart of Christianity is a myth which is also a fact."[1]

In other words, we all dream about a perfect period in the world because there truly is a better world available. We not only know this in our hearts, but we also know it from our Bibles. There is a better world coming! But I'm not speaking about heaven yet; I'm talking about a better world on planet Earth itself.

In this study guide we are going to explore what the Bible says about a coming Golden Age when a great and glorious King will rule over a happy planet filled with noble people. Revelation 19 describes the return of Christ and the defeat of the Antichrist at the battle of Armageddon. Then we turn the page, and Revelation 20:1–4 tells us that Satan is going to be bound for a thousand years and that Christ will reign for that same thousand years over the earth. Christ is going to reign over this earth for a millennium, a thousand years, and it is going to be a good experience!

After the return of Jesus Christ in the Rapture, where we will rise to meet the Lord in the air, the earth will endure seven years of tribulation, leading to the battle of Armageddon. That's when Jesus will appear as lightning in the sky, returning to the Mount of Olives, entering the city of Jerusalem, and establishing His kingdom.

We focus a lot of attention on the second coming of Christ, but most people don't know a lot about His subsequent reign on earth. It's not something to be skimmed over, especially since there's more prophetic Scripture about the Millennium than any other subject. J. Dwight Pentecost wrote, "This millennial age, in which the purposes of God are fully realized on the earth, demands considerable attention."[2]

During this time, life on earth will be as it was intended for us before the Fall and introduction of sin in the garden of Eden. This epoch where Christ reigns on this planet will reverse all the curses that happened after Adam and Eve disobeyed God. This will be a world like no other world.

For instance, the book of Isaiah tells us it is going to be a time of happiness: "For you shall go out with joy, and be led out with peace; the mountains and the hills shall break forth into singing before you, and all the trees of the field shall clap their hands" (Isaiah 55:12). Earlier in the same book, we are told that it will be a time of global peace: "They shall beat their swords into plowshares, and their spears into pruning hooks; nation shall not lift up sword against nation, neither shall they learn war anymore" (Isaiah 2:4).

The Bible says we will study war no more. There will be no more armories or guns. We will take all of these things and turn them into implements of agriculture. Can you imagine a world without the threat of war? A world that's at peace, where men and women don't fight with each other over the simple things of life? What a wonderful time that will be!

The coming Golden Age will also be a time marked by prosperity: "The open pastures are springing up, and the tree bears its fruit; the fig tree and the vine yield their strength. . . . The threshing floors shall be full of wheat, and the vats shall overflow with new wine and oil" (Joel 2:22, 24). Prosperity in biblical times was marked in terms of agriculture, so that is how Joel expressed this coming abundance.

The Millennium will also be defined by a time of harmony in nature. Isaiah 11:6, 9 says, "The wolf also shall dwell with the lamb, the leopard shall lie down with the young goat.... They shall not hurt nor destroy in all My holy mountain." This will be such a time of absolute peace that even the animals will get along with each other!

And this peaceful age will lead to spiritual revival: "They shall not hurt nor destroy in all My holy mountain, for the earth shall be full of the knowledge of the LORD as the waters cover the sea" (Isaiah 11:9).

Now, as incredible as all those descriptions of that time may be, the most surprising aspect of the coming Golden Age is that many of us have been praying for it since we were children, though we may not have realized it. The millennial kingdom of Jesus Christ will be the ultimate fulfillment of the prayer taught to us by Jesus: "Our Father in heaven, hallowed be Your name. Your kingdom come. Your will be done on earth as it is in heaven" (Matthew 6:9–10).

Each and every day, millions of Christians utter the Lord's Prayer in hundreds of languages and in thousands of diverse settings and situations. This has been the case for the last 2,000 years. No prayer has been more frequently spoken, more meaningfully offered, and more urgently needed than the prayer that Jesus taught us. Even now, as you read this lesson, someone somewhere is praying the sixty-six words of the Lord's Prayer.

I would like to suggest that when we pray, "Your kingdom come," we are praying for two parallel realties: we are praying for the kingdom of God to come into our hearts, and we are praying for the kingdom of God to come on earth—that time we refer to as the Millennium—the coming Golden Age.

There are two phases to the coming of our Lord's kingdom.

The Kingdom of Grace

The first kingdom is the present reality that we live in and is simply called the kingdom of grace. Today, as the church of the Lord Jesus Christ, we are part of God's kingdom, but that kingdom lives in our hearts. We are under the King of heaven, and His kingdom is in our hearts.

There is a certain and specific phrase that biblical scholars use to describe the kingdom of God: "Already but not yet." The idea is that while the kingdom of heaven is already here in our hearts, it is not here on earth yet in its physical fullness. One of these days when Jesus comes back and the Tribulation is over, Christ will set up His kingdom on this planet, and it will be the ultimate fulfillment of the Lord's Prayer, "Your kingdom come."

The Word of God says that the kingdom of God is our present spiritual reality. Those of us who know Jesus Christ as our Lord are, at this very moment, citizens of the kingdom of God on this earth. We are walking models of those who have allowed the Lord to reign on the throne of our hearts. We are kingdom people, infiltrating the earth for His purposes.

Jesus began His preaching ministry with the news of the imminent appearing of the kingdom of God. He said, "Repent, for the kingdom of heaven is at hand" (Matthew 4:17). He also said, "Let the little children come to Me, and do not forbid them; for of such is the kingdom of God" (Mark 10:14). In Luke 17:21, He said, "The kingdom of God is within you," and when He stood before Pilate, He said, "My kingdom is not of this world. If My kingdom were of this world, My servants would fight" (John 18:36). Jesus made it very clear the kingdom was not yet to be a physical kingdom; it was in a time yet to come. At the same time, it is an inheritance which God will provide for all of us who are Christians. All Christians will go into the Millennium.

The word "kingdom" means "the king's domain." If you acknowledge Jesus Christ today, you're in His kingdom. You acknowledge that the King of heaven, King Jesus, is in charge of your life, and you do His will.

When the Holy Spirit descended on the 120 disciples in the upper room in Jerusalem shortly after the ascension of Christ, the church came into existence. And this great kingdom of God, which is spread all over the world, made up of believers of every nation and tongue, continues to grow, and we will all one day enter into the kingdom where King Jesus will literally and physically be our King.

So when you pray, "Your kingdom come. Your will be done on earth as it is in heaven," this is a petition for God to reign. When you pray for God's kingdom on earth, you are praying for the spreading of the Gospel and the expansion of the church. This could take the form of missionaries abroad or local churches just down the street. Whenever you intercede and echo the prayer of Christ, you are asking God to let His kingdom come to all the earth, and it will be like nothing you can imagine.

The Kingdom of Glory

Then we have the kingdom of glory. Even though Jesus spoke extensively about the kingdom of grace, He had even more in mind when He taught us to pray, "Your kingdom come." For this petition cannot be perfectly fulfilled by the present era of the church. In the upper room, Jesus told His disciples, "And I bestow upon you a kingdom, just as My Father bestowed one upon Me, that you may eat and drink at My table in My kingdom, and sit on thrones judging the twelve tribes of Israel" (Luke 22:29–30).

The phrase "My kingdom" means not only the kingdom of grace, which is in our hearts, but also the kingdom of glory coming after the Tribulation when King Jesus will be on this earth. It will be a time of spirituality. In fact, Satan won't be here! For one thousand years, Satan will be locked up in the bottomless pit. He will have no way of escape and no influence over anything that happens in the Millennium. There will still be sin, but it won't be because of Satan's influence over us. This proves that we have sinful natures that cause us to do things we shouldn't do, even when Satan isn't a factor.

In that day, the kingdoms of this world will become the kingdoms of the Lord and of Christ. He will reign for a thousand years, and everyone who is a Christian will enter into that kingdom and be with Him. In fact, at the beginning there will be no unbelievers on the earth. Psalm 145:11–12 says, "They shall speak of the glory of Your kingdom, and talk of Your power, to make known to the sons of men His mighty acts, and the glorious majesty of His kingdom."

The prophet Obadiah described that moment as follows: "The day of the LORD upon all the nations is near. . . . But on Mount Zion there shall be deliverance, and there shall be holiness; the house of Jacob shall possess their possessions. . . . And the kingdom shall be the LORD's" (Obadiah 15, 17, 21).

We should think of this whenever we look at the map. Today we have immense countries like Russia, which spreads from central Europe to furthest Asia. The United States rests between the Atlantic and Pacific Oceans. Among the smallest nations of the world is tiny Israel, only about ten miles at its narrowest point and a mere 263 miles from north to south. Yet this tiny country will be the power center of the entire globe during the kingdom of glory. When that prophecy is fulfilled, the boundaries of Israel will stretch from the Mediterranean Sea to the Euphrates River (see Joshua 1:4), and Zion will be the capital of the world (see Psalm 2:6). Jesus will reign from His throne, and all the nations will fall into place under His authority. Peace will reign, God's holy people will populate the government, and a scepter of righteousness will be the scepter of His kingdom (see Hebrews 1:8).

According to Mark Hitchcock, "The millennial kingdom will have no need for rescue missions, welfare programs, food stamps, or relief agencies. The world will flourish under the hand of the King of heaven."[3]

Dr. M. R. DeHaan wrote of this day:

> The Bible is replete with prophecies of a coming age of peace and prosperity. It will be a time when war will be utterly unknown. Not a single armament plant will be operating, not a soldier or sailor will be in uniform, no military camps will exist, and not one cent will be spent for armaments of war, not a single penny will be used for defense, much less for offensive warfare. Can you imagine such an age, when all nations shall be at perfect peace, all the resources available for enjoyment, all industry engaged in the articles of a peaceful luxury?[4]

Whenever you pray the Lord's Prayer, you're praying for that kingdom to come.

The venerable J. Vernon McGee put it like this: "The Millennium is God's answer to the prayer, 'Thy kingdom come.' When we pray . . . the Lord's Prayer, we say, 'Thy kingdom come . . . in earth, as it is in heaven' (Matthew 6:10). That is the kingdom which He is going to establish here on earth, and it is called the Millennium."[5] Just as the angels in the invisible realms honor and quickly obey their King, so will it be on this planet. So it should be with you and me now.

Back in the 1970s, Bill and Gloria Gaither were busy with family and life. One evening they entertained two friends who told them about a sermon they'd heard from a preacher named Jim Crabtree. Crabtree was so excited about the return of Christ that he ended his sermon by walking through the congregation shouting, "The King is coming! The King is coming! The King is coming!"

After their friends left, Bill and Gloria kept talking about the glorious moment when the King will come amidst a glorious coronation processional. Bill sat down at the piano and composed a melody while Gloria wrote the lyrics to the now well-known song "The King Is Coming."

Yes, the King is coming, but so is the kingdom! And the Bible gives us three prayers about this kingdom that we can pray as we look forward to that day. The first one has been emphasized throughout this study, straight from the Lord's Prayer: "Your kingdom come. Your will be done on earth as it is in heaven" (Matthew 6:10).

The second prayer is a one-word term that may be familiar to those of you who grew up reading the King James Version of the Bible. The apostle Paul closed his first letter to the Corinthians with the word "Maranatha" (1 Corinthians 16:22 KJV). This word means, "O Lord, come!" Paul used it as an exclamatory request to heaven for the soon return of Jesus Christ to set up His kingdom of glory.

The third prayer is very similar to that of "Maranatha" and is the final prayer of the Bible found in Revelation 22:20: "Even so, come, Lord Jesus!" This should be the prayer of every believer in every season of life. It should come to our minds when we face trials and temptations of all kinds. It should sound from our hearts whenever we see a beautiful sunrise. In all seasons, we should pray for the speedy and soon return of our Lord.

We don't always have an appreciation for the things that are going to happen in the future, but let me tell you something—they're going to happen anyway! The more we can learn about God's great kingdom plan, the more we can understand what's happening and be a little more patient. This has never been the world God wanted us to have. This is a world tainted with the sin of mankind. But there's a coming world where there will be no sin, no crime, no poverty, and no sickness. In that coming world, death will happen very rarely, and the Bible says that during that time, a person who's a hundred years old will be considered a child. That's what God has in store for us.

As Christians, we know that someday we will reign with Him in His literal earthly kingdom. But right now, He's in our heart, and until His kingdom of glory comes to this earth, we must ask Him to help us live our lives as we would when that kingdom has come. May we always have a heart to pray for the kingdom to come. "Maranatha! Even so, come, Lord Jesus! Your kingdom come. Your will be done on earth as it is in heaven."

APPLICATION

Personal Questions

1. Read Isaiah 55:12 and 2:4. What do these verses tell you about the coming Golden Age?

2. Read Matthew 6:9–10.

    a. How do these verses change for you now that you know they refer to the coming Golden Age?

    b. What are we praying for?

3. What are the two phases to the coming of our Lord's kingdom?

    a. The kingdom of _____.

    b. The kingdom of _____.

4. Briefly explain the kingdom of grace, including the idea of "already but not yet."

5. Read Matthew 4:17, Mark 10:14, Luke 17:21, and John 18:36. After reading these verses, what do you think Jesus is telling us about the imminent appearing of the kingdom of God?

6. What does the word "kingdom" mean? In this context, what does it mean to acknowledge Jesus Christ in your life?

7. Read Luke 22:29–30. In these verses, Jesus refers to the kingdom of grace and to the kingdom of glory. Briefly explain the kingdom of glory.

8. What influence will Satan have during the coming Golden Age, and why? Does this change the idea of sin during the Millennium? How so?

9. Read Joshua 1:4, Psalm 2:6, and Hebrews 1:8. What do these verses tell you about the country of Israel during the kingdom of glory?

10. Read 1 Corinthians 16:22 (in the King James Version, if you can). What does the word "Maranatha" mean?

11. Write out each of these verses, and then combine them into the prayer that should be on the lips of every believer.

   a. Matthew 6:10:

   b. 1 Corinthians 16:22 (the meaning):

   c. Revelation 22:20:

Group Questions

1. Read Joel 2:22, 24 and Isaiah 11:6, 9.

   a. In addition to happiness and peace, discuss the other three descriptors that will define the Millennium.

b. We hear different theories about whether or not animals will be in heaven. If the Millennium is a prelude to heaven, discuss what Isaiah 11:6 might indicate.

2. As a group, read Matthew 6:9–10. Based on this lesson, what are these verses specifically referring to? Discuss how this knowledge might change the way you think about this prayer.

3. Together, discuss the difference between the kingdom of grace and the kingdom of glory, including the idea of "already but not yet."

4. Discuss the meaning of the word "kingdom" and what it means to someone who is a Christian.

5. After studying this lesson, discuss why it's important to study the coming Golden Age.

DID YOU KNOW?

The phrase "already but not yet" that has been made famous to describe the kingdom of God was coined more than a hundred years ago by a Dutch American theologian named Geerhardus Vos. He was the first Professor of Biblical Theology at Princeton Theological Seminary. He was also a master of languages, fluent in German, Dutch, Latin, French, English, Greek, and Hebrew! While Vos was the first to term the phrase "already but not yet," it was made popular in the 1950s by another man, George Eldon Ladd, who was a Baptist minister and a longtime professor at Fuller Theological Seminary.

Notes
1. C. S. Lewis, *Miracles* (San Francisco, CA: HarperOne, 2009), 176.
2. J. Dwight Pentecost, *Things to Come: A Study in Biblical Eschatology* (Grand Rapids, MI: Zondervan, 1958), 476.
3. Mark Hitchcock, *The End* (Carol Stream, IL: Tyndale, 2012), 428.
4. Dr. M. R. DeHaan, *The Great Society* (Radio Bible Class, 1965), 7–8.
5. J. Vernon McGee, Thru the Bible Commentary Series, volume 60: The Prophecy—Revelation 14–22 (Nashville, TN: Thomas Nelson, 1991).

LESSON 2

THE GOLDEN CITY

JEREMIAH 3:17

In this lesson we learn about God's chosen city, Jerusalem, and its role in the coming Golden Age.

The city of Jerusalem is featured prominently in the Bible—mentioned more than 800 times. In today's society we often hear of the events that occur within and around that city. Still, there is much more in store for the future of Jerusalem. Studying Jerusalem's role in the coming Golden Age is important, for when Christ returns, the city will be changed, and during the Millennium, it is the place from which Christ will reign.

OUTLINE

I. **A Conflicted City**

II. **A Chosen City**

III. **A Christ-Loved City**

IV. **A Changed City**

V. A Capital City

VI. A Continuing City

VII. A Challenging City
    A. Determine to Love Israel
    B. Determine to Learn from Israel

OVERVIEW

Eliezer Ben-Yehuda and his new wife, Deborah, sailed wide-eyed into the port of Joppa, which is in northern Israel. They had dreamed that one day they would be able to step into the Holy Land, and now their dream had come true. They arranged to get from Joppa to Jerusalem by an overnight horse cart, and they approached the city just as the sun was coming up. They noticed that the gate had been closed to the city, but just as they got there, it started to open. It seemed almost miraculous to them. But when they entered into the city, they were very confused.

They thought, *Where are the Jerusalem people? Where is the spirit of holiness we expected? Was this the city that had so many centuries of conflict and plunder and massacre and misery? Was this the city from which men from all over the world had fought? Was this the city that the prophets had preached about and that had been destroyed and reconstructed eighteen times?*[1]

The city didn't seem right.

You see, the year was 1881. And Eliezer and Deborah were among the first Zionist Jews returning to the land that later would once again be called Israel. In the years to come, Ben-Yehuda would almost singlehandedly do the impossible—resurrect the Hebrew language from antiquity and make it the language of the Jews once again.

In fact, Eliezer and Deborah had a son, Ben, and they told Ben that he would never hear another language in their house except Hebrew. Growing up, he did not know any other language but Hebrew. It was spoken every day. And Ben-Zion was raised hearing and speaking only Hebrew; he became the first native speaker of Hebrew in modern times.

Eliezer and his wife believed if their own son could learn the language, the whole nation could learn the language.

Now fast-forward to one of my more recent visits to Israel. Donna and I were shopping on Ben Yehuda Street. Everyone said the street was the best street in Jerusalem, so I started asking questions. And a friend got me a book on the life story of Eliezer Ben-Yehuda. It's the story of him and his wife and family digging out the remnants of the old Hebrew language and putting it back together so that the Jewish people would have their own natural tongue.

They went to museums all over Europe hunting for just one word. And God used that family to restore the Hebrew language to the Jewish people.

Sadly, Ben-Yehuda didn't live long enough to see the state of Israel become official. It was 1948 when Israel officially became a nation, and the United States was the first nation to recognize the statehood of Israel.

But Yehuda and his wife were very popular people, very loved people because of the gift they had given to the nation. When he died, 30,000 people came to his funeral, and he was buried on the Mount of Olives.

So what drew the Zionists back to Jerusalem? Why is Israel today filled with excitement, even though there's war and all kinds of things going on there? Why is it such a magnetic place?

A Conflicted City

Jerusalem is a very conflicted city.

For 3,000 years, it's been at the forefront of geopolitical struggles. Even today, it's the centerpiece of the world's three major religions. It's ground zero for international political maneuvering. For generations, Jerusalem has been a place of pilgrimage and pillaging, miracles and mayhem. They're shot at from the north and shot at from the south; rockets come in from everywhere. They are hated by many of their neighbors but are loved and respected by many of us. Teddy Kollek, the longtime mayor of Jerusalem, said, "Jerusalem has been the center of Jewish hope and longing. No other city has played such a dominant role in the history, culture, religion, and consciousness of a people as Jerusalem in the life of Jewry and Judaism."[2]

So when we talk about Jerusalem, we must remember that it's much more than just a city in the Middle East.

A Chosen City

Jerusalem is a chosen city.

Why does this desert city charm people when they go there?

Whenever I go to Israel, we start out in the northern part of the country by the Sea of Galilee, where we stay in Tiberius for a little bit. Then we come down, and we spend three to five days in Jerusalem. We stay in a hotel right in the center of the city, and periodically when I go out of that hotel to walk around in the city, I feel like I'm under some sort of a spell. It's like an aura that surrounds you. I never understood that until I began to really read what the Scripture says about Jerusalem.

The Bible tells us that Jerusalem has a big badge on it that says, "God's City." Second Chronicles 6:5–6 says, "Since the day that I brought My people out of the land of Egypt, I have chosen no city from any tribe of Israel in which to build a house, that My name might be there, nor did I choose any man to be a ruler over My people Israel. Yet I have chosen Jerusalem, that My name may be there."

The reason Jerusalem is special to me is because it's God's chosen city. Of all the cities of the world, and there are many, God chose Jerusalem as His city. And because it is God who established the city, Psalm 87:3 says, "O city of God, what glorious things are said of you!" (NLT).

You may not realize how prominent this city is in the Bible. It's mentioned 811 times. The next closest city is mentioned only a couple hundred times. And the Bible intimates that if you are born in Jerusalem, there's a special blessing attached to you. Psalm 87:5–6 says, "Someday the highest honor will be to be a native of Jerusalem! For the God above all gods will personally bless this city. When he registers her citizens, he will place a check mark beside the names of those who were born here" (TLB).

So if you are born in Jerusalem, God puts a check mark next to your name. I don't understand all that, but I believe it. And I know it's just another reminder to us of the importance of Jerusalem, and a reminder to us that we should learn everything we can about this city as we head toward the future.

A Christ-Loved City

And it's a city that was loved by Christ.

I put it this way—Jesus was a Jerusalem boy. He loved Jerusalem. He first visited the city as an infant when He was dedicated to the Lord in the temple. Then when He was twelve years old, Jesus went to Jerusalem again during the Passover. He didn't want to come home, so He stayed three days longer. His parents left and didn't know that He wasn't with them. They were almost home when one of them said, "Where's Jesus?" And they realized that they had left Him in Jerusalem. When they found Him, He was sitting among the teachers answering all of their questions like He was an adult.

When Jesus was baptized, He was taken to Jerusalem. He and others around Him spent many days in Jerusalem. He was arrested in Jerusalem. He was tried in Jerusalem. He was crucified in Jerusalem. He was buried in Jerusalem. He was resurrected in Jerusalem. He ascended from Jerusalem. And one day He's coming back to Jerusalem, and He's going to put His feet on the same place from which He ascended, the Mount of Olives.

Jesus loved Jerusalem. There's no question about it. We read of Jesus' lament over Jerusalem. He said, "O Jerusalem, Jerusalem, the one who kills the prophets and stones those who are sent to her! How often I wanted to gather your children together, as a hen gathers her chicks under her wings, but you were not willing!" (Matthew 23:37)

A Changed City

Jerusalem is a conflicted city, a chosen city, a Christ-loved city, but it's also a city that's going to be changed.

That brings us to the Golden Age—the Millennium. Three things are going to happen in Jerusalem when Jesus' feet touch Mount Olivet.

First, when He comes back and His feet touch the ground, He will trigger an amazing earthquake. This is spoken of several times in the Bible. Zechariah 14:4 says, "And in that day His feet will stand on the Mount of Olives, which faces Jerusalem on the east. And the Mount of Olives shall be split in two."

The Mount of Olives is a 2.2-mile-long ridge on the eastern flanks of Jerusalem. And every time I take groups to the Holy Land, we stand on the Mount of Olives and look out over the Kidron Valley at the golden walls surrounding the old city. It's one of the most beautiful sites in the whole world, and it's a breathtaking view as you stand on the Mount of Olives and see Jerusalem on the horizon.

But an earthquake is not all that's going to happen. That earthquake is going to form an escape route for the Jews in Jerusalem who will need to get out of the city, and it will also be a place where aquifers from underground will erupt and form a river.

Zechariah tells us: "On that day living water will flow out from Jerusalem, half of it east to the Dead Sea and half of it west to the Mediterranean Sea, in summer and in winter" (14:8 NIV). In other words, the river will divide at some point south of Jerusalem. Half of it will go to the Mediterranean Sea, and the other half will go to the Dead Sea, where it will transform the Dead Sea from a dead sea to a living sea. If you've ever been to Israel and to the Dead Sea, you know it's the lowest point on the earth. And the Dead Sea is called the Dead Sea because nothing lives in it.

The prophet Ezekiel devotes an entire chapter to describing this in his book. He said, "I saw water coming out from under the threshold of the temple toward the east" (47:1 NIV). And then, according to Ezekiel, this river will grow stronger and wider. "This water flows toward the eastern region and goes down into the Arabah, where it enters the Dead Sea. When it empties into the sea, the salty water there becomes fresh. Swarms of living creatures will live wherever the river flows. There will be large numbers of fish, because this water flows there and makes the salt water fresh" (47:8–9 NIV).

According to Ezekiel, there will be a day in the Millennium where the Dead Sea will be a fishing paradise. "Fishermen will stand along the shore; from En Gedi to En Eglaim there will be places for spreading nets. The fish will be of many kinds—like the fish of the Mediterranean Sea. . . . Fruit trees of all kinds will grow on both banks of the river. Their leaves will not wither, nor will their fruit fail" (verses 10, 12 NIV).

Can you imagine the change that will take place just because Jesus is back with His people and with His angels to set up His kingdom?

But there's more.

The power of Christ's return will trigger an earthquake, it will unleash a river, it will precipitate a geological change in the Dead Sea, and it will also elevate the city of Jerusalem as though it were on an elevator. The entire city will be lifted up, and everyone will look to the city.

Isaiah hinted at this when he said, "Now it shall come to pass in the latter days that the mountain of the LORD's house shall be established on the top of the mountains, and shall be exalted above the hills; and all nations shall flow to it" (2:2).

Chapter 14 of Zechariah gives even more specific details: "The whole land, from Geba to Rimmon, south of Jerusalem, will become like the Arabah. But Jerusalem will be raised up high from the Benjamin Gate to the site of the First Gate, to the Corner Gate, and from the Tower . . . and will remain in its place. It will be inhabited; never again will it be destroyed. Jerusalem will be secure" (verses 10–11 NIV).

These verses tell us on that day, the Lord will bring to Jerusalem and her surrounding regions an elevation of the city of Jerusalem that will make it the highest city in the world. The area on top of Jerusalem will be ten miles, and Ezekiel's temple will be created on the top of that mountain. The Lord will lower the elevation of the rest of the city of Jerusalem, and it will be like the desert. But out of the midst of this desert will rise up this incredible mountain upon which will be the city of Jerusalem and the temple of Ezekiel.

What an amazing thing is going to happen when Jesus comes back.

In other words, the very geography of the promised land is going to be altered at the second coming of Christ. The Mount of Olives will be fractured, opening a wide and accessible lane for the residents to flee the city for safer places. The foundation of the city will shift to such a degree that rivers of healing water will flow throughout the city. And the elevation of the city will rise as the surrounding countryside levels out.

Why is all this going to take place?

Because the King has returned. Jerusalem will no longer be a fortress surrounded by people who want to take it out. It will be a beacon on a hill, elevated over large, flat plains, an invitation to come and see the King.

Let me suggest that in a spiritual sense, what happens when Jesus comes back to set up His reign and rule in Jerusalem is what happens to us when Jesus comes to set up His reign and rule in our hearts. When we let Jesus sit on the throne of our lives, He creates living water flowing from us. John 7 says, "'Let anyone who is thirsty come to me and drink. Whoever believes in me, as Scripture has said, rivers of living water will flow from within them.' By this he meant the Spirit, whom those who believed in him were later to receive" (verses 37–39 NIV).

On the day you were saved, God shook you up. And you should allow what He's doing in your life to have its perfect way, so that wherever you go, you take with you the influence of the Lord Jesus Christ.

A Capital City

The Bible says that God blesses those who bless Israel and curses those who curse Israel.

One day, Israel, which is so criticized by everybody, will become the capital of the whole world. Jerusalem is the capital of Israel now. But the prophet Jeremiah said that when Jesus comes back and He sets up His kingdom, "they will call Jerusalem The Throne of the LORD, and all nations will gather in Jerusalem to honor the name of the LORD" (3:17 NIV).

And Zechariah said, "Many nations shall be joined to the LORD in that day, and they shall become My people. And I will dwell in your midst. Then you will know that the LORD of hosts has sent Me to you. And the LORD will take possession of Judah as His inheritance in the Holy Land, and will again choose Jerusalem" (2:11–12).

Even though it doesn't seem like it, Jerusalem is at the center of our world. Without Jerusalem, none of the things the Bible says are going to happen will happen. Jerusalem is the place that God has put His finger on. It is His chosen city. It is the city of God.

A Continuing City

Jerusalem is a changed city, it is a capital city, and it's a continuing city.

Almost all the Christ-centered events in the future will take place in Jerusalem. Without Jerusalem, these events would be impossible.

I remember when the state of Israel was established in 1948, and Jewish people returned to their land. It was like somebody turned a key in the prophetic clock and opened the door to a lot more things than what we had known before.

I believe that when the U.S. embassy moved back to Jerusalem in 2017, another key was turned in the prophetic clock. We are seeing things happen in our day that have never happened before. We read about them in the Bible, and it's an amazing journey to watch God unfold the future of the Middle East, just as He promised He would.

So the city of Jerusalem has a great future. One day Jesus will be seated on the throne, and the whole world will be under His subjection. The Bible teaches that the city of Jerusalem will be the capital of the whole world.

A Challenging City

I want to conclude this lesson with two challenges for all of us.

Determine to Love Israel

First of all, in our hearts, no matter who we are or what our background is, if we're Christians, we need to determine to love Israel. We should determine to love Israel and its capital city. Here's what the psalmist said: "Pray for the peace of Jerusalem: 'May they prosper who love you. Peace be within your walls, prosperity within your palaces.' For the sake of my brethren and companions, I will now say, 'Peace be within you.' Because of the house of the LORD our God I will seek your good" (Psalm 122:6-9).

There is some instruction for us about what our attitude should be about Jerusalem and what our attitude should be about the Jewish people. God prospers those who love Jerusalem. So when you pray, make sure Israel is on your prayer list. Pray for the international safety of Israel.

Modern Israel has been forced to maintain a continual state of warfare throughout its years. Someone has said Israel is like living in a very nice house in a very bad neighborhood. And that's where they are. And they need our prayers.

Determine to Learn from Israel

Secondly, there's a lot we can learn from Jerusalem and from Israel.

Joseph Lieberman, who was a U.S. senator, ran for vice president in 2000 and became the first Jewish candidate to ever be on a presidential ticket. He wrote a book called *The Gift of Rest: Rediscovering the Beauty of the Sabbath*. And he said, "I love the Sabbath and believe it is a gift from God that I want to share with everyone." He continued, "When people ask me: 'How can you stop all your work as a senator to observe the Sabbath each week?' I answer, 'How could I do all my work as a senator if I did not stop to observe the Sabbath each week?'"

Lieberman wrote, "The truth is that we—and the world—will survive just fine if we stop working or shopping and stay home with our families one a day each week. Our lives will continue. Our careers will go forward. Our families will flourish.

"We live in a culture of hard work where people are desperately in need of rest—not just rest to recharge our batteries so we can work harder but to recharge our souls so we can live better. For me, the answer to that need has been the Sabbath. It has anchored my life, revived my body, and restored my soul. I know the Sabbath can do the same for you."[3]

As Christians, we don't observe the Sabbath. We observe the Lord's Day. But many of the things that are said about the Sabbath could surely be said about the Lord's Day. When we set aside time to go and honor the Lord, we not only honor the Lord, but the Lord also honors us.

If you want God to bless you in your life, be a man or a woman of the church. The Bible tells us not to forsake the assembling of ourselves together (see Hebrews 10:25). And we should especially obey that command as we see the day of the Lord drawing near.

The local church should be crucial to us as God's people. And even more so because we live on the other side of the cross. We know the Messiah has come, and as we have been learning, He's coming again. When He comes again, He will set all things right. And we will live for one thousand years under the reign of King Jesus.

APPLICATION

Personal Questions

1. What do you know about the city of Jerusalem from Scripture and from history and current events?

2. Read 2 Chronicles 6:5–6. Why did God choose Jerusalem, according to these verses?

3. Read Psalm 87:3–6. What does this passage tell us about those who are born in Jerusalem?

4. Read Luke 2:21–24, 41–50.

   a. When did Jesus first visit Jerusalem with Joseph and Mary?

   b. Explain what happened when Jesus visited Jerusalem for the Passover when He was twelve years old.

5. Read Zechariah 14:4, 8–11, and Ezekiel 47:1–12.

    a. How will the geography of Jerusalem change at Christ's second coming?

    b. How will these changes impact areas outside of Jerusalem?

6. According to Zechariah 2:11–12 and Jeremiah 3:17, what will happen in Jerusalem during the Millennium? How is this radically different from how Jerusalem is treated by the world today?

7. What does Psalm 122:6–9 challenge us to do for the city of Jerusalem?

8. What steps can you take to make Sunday more of a day of rest in your life? Choose one step to implement in the coming week.

Group Questions

1. Discuss together what you know about Jerusalem from Scripture, as well as from world history and current events.

2. Read 2 Chronicles 6:5–6 and Psalm 87:3–6. What do these two passages teach us about the city of Jerusalem?

3. As a group, list as many events as you can think of from the life of Christ that took place in Jerusalem.

4. Read Matthew 23:37 together and discuss the importance of Jerusalem to Christ.

5. Read Zechariah 14:4, 8–11, and Ezekiel 47:1–12 as a group.

   a. Discuss the geographical changes that will occur in Jerusalem and in other parts of Israel at Christ's second coming.

   b. What is the reason for these geographical changes?

6. What will be Jerusalem's role in the coming Golden Age?

7. Discuss the Jewish law of keeping the Sabbath. Although we don't keep the Sabbath as Christians, what are practical ways we can make Sunday, the Lord's Day, a day of worship and rest for ourselves and our families?

8. Psalm 122:6–9 tells us to "pray for the peace of Jerusalem." Take a few moments to write down some specific requests for the city and the people who call it home. Then spend time praying together for Jerusalem.

DID YOU KNOW?

Despite war and unrest in Israel, the city of Jerusalem has more than one million residents. More than 60% of its "residents were Jews or classified as 'others,'" while close to 40% were Arabs. More than 90% of the city's residents "considered themselves satisfied with their lives, and 87% of residents considered themselves satisfied with their work."[4] While those who live in Jerusalem now are satisfied with their lives and work, just think of how much more satisfied with life and work Jerusalem residents will be during the coming Golden Age!

Notes

1. Robert St. John, *Tongue of the Prophets: The Life Story of Ben-Yehuda* (Noble, OK: Balfour Books, 2013), Kindle location 1215–1227.
2. Teddy Kollek, *Jerusalem* (Washington, DC: Washington Institute for Near East Policy, 1990), 19–20.
3. Joe Lieberman, *The Gift of Rest: Rediscovering the Beauty of the Sabbath* (New York, NY: Howard Books, 2011), opening note, 34, 221.
4. "Jerusalem's Population Reaches One Million Residents in 2024," *The Jerusalem Post*, June 6, 2024, https://www.jpost.com/israel-news/article-805171.

LESSON 3

KING JESUS

ZECHARIAH 14:9

In this lesson we explore the different aspects of the absolute authority Jesus holds as King.

In Matthew 1:21, Joseph is told in a dream that Mary will have a son conceived of the Holy Spirit and that His name will be Jesus, meaning "the Lord is salvation." He would be the Messiah, and throughout the Old and New Testaments, He would be called by many different titles, each referring to a different aspect of His authority. Exploring these varied titles helps us to better understand King Jesus and His reign during the coming Golden Age.

OUTLINE

I. The Redeeming King
   A. King of the Jews
   B. King of Israel
   C. King of Kings

    D. King over All the Earth
    E. King of Glory

II. The Reigning King
    A. His Kingdom Is Universal
    B. His Kingdom Is Physical
    C. His Kingdom Is Spiritual
    D. His Kingdom Is Ethical
    E. His Kingdom Is Eternal

OVERVIEW

Queen Elizabeth II was the longest-reigning monarch in the history of British royalty. When she passed away in 2022, the whole world paused at the word of her death. She had a tremendous presence and influence throughout the globe.

And with the tremendous platform that was afforded to her, she spoke about her faith in Christ. In her 2011 Christmas broadcast, she said, "Jesus was born into a world full of fear. The angels came to frightened shepherds with hope in their voices: 'Fear not.'"

In that same broadcast, she said, "It is through this lens of history that we should view the conflicts of today, and so give us hope for tomorrow."[1]

What she said there is true, but let's change just one word in that sentence. I want to suggest that "it is through the lens of *prophecy* that we should view the conflicts of today, and so give us hope for tomorrow."

History is important, and the Christian faith is grounded in historical facts like the death, burial, and resurrection of Jesus Christ. But anyone can look backward. The only ones who can truly peer into the future are those who study what God has said in Scripture. We can know what will happen in the coming days only if we will examine God's Word.

The same Jesus who died and rose from the dead will come again and reign over this world. But He will reign far longer than Elizabeth II—who occupied the British throne for a remarkable seventy years and 214 days. Imagine a King who will occupy His throne on this planet for one thousand years!

Understanding the return of Christ and His millennial reign is what will help us understand the conflicts of today and give us hope for tomorrow.

The Bible presents Jesus not just as Savior, Messiah, and Friend, but it also declares Jesus as King. And at this very moment, Christ Jesus is already in heaven sitting on the throne at the right hand of the Father, making intercession for us. Even as we enthrone Him as King in our hearts now, one day He will literally be King over all the earth. So let's examine the glory, majesty, power, and authority of King Jesus and His kingdom.

The Redeeming King

Jesus is a redeeming King, and all these depictions and portrayals of Jesus as King come straight from Scripture.

King of the Jews

What is interesting about Jesus' title as King of the Jews is that it was only used during two periods of His life—at His birth in Bethlehem and at the end of His life in Jerusalem. Oddly, this phrase occurs nowhere in the Old Testament, nor do we find it in the epistles. It occurs only in the Gospels at the birth and death of our Lord.

After Jesus was born, the wise men came from the East, asking, "Where is He who has been born King of the Jews? For we have seen His star in the East and have come to worship Him" (Matthew 2:2). Years later, at age thirty-three, Jesus stood before the governor, Pontius Pilate, who asked Him, "Are You the King of the Jews?" Jesus replied, "It is as you say" (Matthew 27:11).

Addressing the mob before him, Pilate shouted, "Do you want me to release to you the King of the Jews? . . . What then do you want me to do with Him whom you call the King of the Jews?" (Mark 15:9, 12) The response of the crowd was, "Crucify Him!" (verse 13).

When Pilate handed over Christ for crucifixion, it came along with a strange order for the executioners. They were instructed to make a sign and nail it to the top of the cross. Mark 15:26 tells us what the sign said: "THE KING OF THE JEWS."

This was our Lord's title, boldly declared at both His birth and His death. It was uttered by the magi, the magistrates, the mob, the markings on His cross, and ultimately by the Master Himself.

King of Israel

The Bible tells us that Jesus is not only the King of the Jews, but He is also the King of Israel. The first person known to have recognized this was the disciple Nathanael, who said in John 1:49, "Rabbi, You are the Son of God! You are the King of Israel!"

Approximately three years later at the Lord's triumphal entry on Palm Sunday, large numbers of people celebrated His arrival in Jerusalem, saying, "Hosanna! 'Blessed is He who comes in the name of the LORD!' The King of Israel!" (John 12:13)

Only five days later, as Jesus suffered on Golgotha, one of His enemies shouted sarcastically, "He saved others; Himself He cannot save. If He is the King of Israel, let Him now come down from the cross, and we will believe Him" (Matthew 27:42). According to this and other Scriptures, Jesus is the only rightful, everlasting heir to the throne of David. Jesus is the King of Israel.

King of Kings

Jesus is also known as the King of kings. This is the Lord's ultimate title of royal honor, as it is beautifully described in the following words: "He has on His robe and on His thigh a name written: KING OF KINGS AND LORD OF LORDS" (Revelation 19:16).

We live in a fallen world full of corrupt leaders who desire supreme authority. But they will never have it—not even the coming Antichrist—for only Jesus is King of kings and Lord of lords. One day every knee will bow before Him, and every tongue will confess that He is Lord.

King over All the Earth

One of the things that surprises people about the coming Golden Age is that it won't just happen in the Middle East. When Jesus sits on the throne in Jerusalem, He will govern the whole world and will oversee everything that happens on the earth. Zechariah 14:9 says, "The LORD shall be King over all the earth. In that day it shall be—'The LORD is one,' and His name one."

King of Glory

The last royal title is found in Psalm 24: "Lift up your heads, O you gates! And be lifted up, you everlasting doors! And the King of glory shall come in. . . . Who is this King of glory? The LORD of hosts, He is the King of glory" (verses 7, 10). The King of glory will be Jesus' millennial title. He's the King of the Jews, the King of Israel, the King of kings, the King over all the earth, and the King of glory. He alone is truly great.

Among the famous figures of history, only a few have been known as "the Great." These characters are like monuments on the pages of time. These were sovereigns who had extraordinary power or left an unusual mark.

From the biblical era, we have Cyrus the Great, Darius the Great, Xerxes the Great, and Herod the Great. Between the Old and New Testaments, the world was changed forever by the meteoric rise of Alexander the Great. Europe also came under the sway of Charlemagne—Charles the Great.

Most of these men were not as great as they thought they were. They were full of failure and sometimes guilty of heinous crimes. And here's the interesting thing: the greatest King in history isn't among them!

Jesus was never called "Jesus the Great" or "Christ the Great." He is great, of course, and greatly to be praised. But His greatness isn't derived from a comparison with other kings. Jesus is in a class by Himself. He stands absolutely alone in history.

He is Jesus the Great, though He doesn't call Himself that—because He doesn't have to. Jesus is the King whose power is absolute, whose reign is infinite, and whose throne is unconquerable. He is an indescribable King, for He reigns eternally without beginning of days or ending of life. He is the epitome of humility, yet the Bible calls Him "the ruler over the kings of the earth" (Revelation 1:5).

He is our Messiah, our Intercessor, the Compassionate Servant, the Humble Teacher, and the Selfless Savior. But never forget He is Christ the King! That title speaks to His sovereignty and indicates that He's in charge of everything. His word is the final word. Nothing can stabilize our emotions like remembering we have a King in heaven who is in charge. Nothing is exempt from His preeminent power. That is why we can call Him the anchor of our soul.

If you're a Christian, Jesus is your Savior. He's a part of your life. But it's one thing to have Him be your Savior and another to have Him be your King. Jesus doesn't just want to be a part of your life; He wants to be the King of your life. And when you put Him on the throne, you're choosing to allow Jesus to take control. One day He'll be our physical King, but for now He wants to be the King of your heart.

The Reigning King

When Jesus came the first time, He came as a redeeming King, establishing a group of people—Jesus followers—over whom He reigns and rules and who do His work on this planet. That is the current kingdom.

But the Bible is full of passages that speak of the kingdom of God in the future tense, when Jesus comes back at the end of the Tribulation and sets up His kingdom on this earth. He is coming as a reigning King, and it is thought that what will happen at that point is a reversal of the curse. If we look back to Genesis, we realize what happened when sin entered the world and the curse was placed on it. As you know, the world in which we live is not the world that God intended for us. If Adam and Eve hadn't sinned, we'd be living in a much better, much different world. That world is coming back, and in the coming Golden Age we'll have the world that we would have had if there had been no sin.

Robert Strauss was a brilliant political strategist who served under several presidents— from Jimmy Carter to George H. W. Bush. He made an interesting statement about the world in which we live: "Everybody in government is like a bunch of ants on a log floating down a river. Each one thinks he is guiding the log, but it is really just going with the flow."[2]

Have you ever noticed the self-importance of many government officials? Everyone seems to think they're running the show. But they're not running the show! They're just going with the flow.

The same can be said of all the rulers of history. All have died or will die, and none has risen from the dead. All of them have dominated the headlines for a period of time, but none has divided history in two like Jesus did. The rulers of this world enjoy limited authority for a limited time. Only Jesus possesses infinite authority for all of eternity. There will never be a time when He is not King.

J. Dwight Pentecost was a seminary professor who wrote a brilliant book entitled *Things to Come*. In one section of the book, he offers a list of the characteristics of Christ's reign as King during the Millennium. Here, with the verses that support them, are just a few of those characteristics.[3]

His Kingdom Is Universal

When Jesus reigns on this earth, His kingdom will be universal. Our Lord's kingdom will be based in the city of Jerusalem, but the Lord's reign will spread northward to Russia, eastward to Asia, and southward to Africa. It will spread westward into Europe, the Americas, and the Pacific Rim. The entire globe will spin under the axis of Jesus. All the nations will sway to His authority.

His Kingdom Is Physical

King Jesus will have an intimate relationship with His subjects. His kingdom will be physical, and nothing expresses that like the way He deals with the infirmities that will enter the kingdom. Consider the words of Isaiah 35:5–6:

> Then the eyes of the blind shall be opened, and the ears of the deaf shall be unstopped. Then the lame shall leap like a deer, and the tongue of the dumb sing. For waters shall burst forth in the wilderness, and streams in the desert.

The miraculous presence of the Lord will change everything. Sickness will be destroyed, and all of the maladies we read about will be nonexistent. Later, Isaiah writes:

> They shall build houses and inhabit them; they shall plant vineyards and eat their fruit. They shall not build and another inhabit; they shall not plant and another eat; for as the days of a tree, so shall be the days of My people, and My elect shall long enjoy the work of their hands" (65:21–22).

The book of Ezekiel talks about topographical changes that will take place in the Middle East, turning the wilderness into a paradise. Even the Dead Sea will be given a pronouncement to become a living lake. Right now, here in our world we're subject to a lot of issues. On the West Coast of the United States there are earthquakes and wildfires. In the central part of our country we have tornados. On the East Coast there are hurricanes. Natural disasters like these can kill hundreds of thousands of people. But during the reign of Christ, we won't have to worry about any of those things. The One who said to the Sea of Galilee in Mark 4:39, "Peace, be still!" will bring peace and stillness to the whole natural world.

His Kingdom Is Spiritual

Jesus' physical reign over the planet will also be a time of spiritual revival. Satan will be bound, and Jesus will be in control. There will be a heart awakening that is unprecedented in human history. According to Zechariah, the entire nation of Israel will return to Jesus:

> And I will pour on the house of David and on the inhabitants of Jerusalem the Spirit of grace and supplication; then they will look on Me whom they pierced. . . . In that day a fountain shall be opened for the house of David and for the inhabitants of Jerusalem, for sin and for uncleanness (12:10; 13:1).

When Jesus is on the throne again, the knowledge of the Lord will fill the land. Everyone will know of the Lord—His name will be on the tongue of all those in the Millennium—His kingdom will be spiritual. Jeremiah says, "No more shall every man teach his neighbor, and every man his brother, saying, 'Know the LORD,' for they all shall know Me, from the least of them to the greatest of them, says the LORD. For I will forgive their iniquity, and their sin I will remember no more" (31:34).

His Kingdom Is Ethical

King Jesus will bring about the return of biblical ethics to our world. Isaiah said this of the coming Golden Age:

> His delight is in the fear of the LORD, and He shall not judge by the sight of His eyes, nor decide by the hearing of His ears; but with righteousness He shall judge the poor, and decide with equity for the meek of the earth; He shall strike the earth with the rod of His mouth, and with the breath of His lips He shall slay the wicked (11:3–4).

The psalmist adds:

> He will judge Your people with righteousness, and Your poor with justice. . . . He will bring justice to the poor of the people; He will save the children of the needy, and will break in pieces

the oppressor. . . . For He will deliver the needy when he cries, the poor also, and him who has no helper. . . . He will redeem their life from oppression and violence; and precious shall be their blood in His sight (Psalm 72:2, 4, 12, 14).

When King Jesus is on the throne, the nation and the world will be filled with the knowledge of the Lord. According to Isaiah, there will even be a road called the "Highway of Holiness" (Isaiah 35:8). And none who are evil can walk on it—only those who love God. Everything about the coming kingdom is holy and righteous.

His Kingdom Is Eternal

The reign of King Jesus will endure a thousand years on earth, but then "the kingdoms of this world [will] become the kingdoms of our Lord" (Revelation 11:15). The end of the thousand-year reign will mark the beginning of our eternity in heaven with Jesus. As Psalm 10:16 says, "The LORD is King forever and ever." This is what we are looking forward to!

We have a King who is never going to outlast Himself. He is never going to be replaced. We don't have to worry about His successor because He doesn't have one. He doesn't have a predecessor either. Jesus is the Holy King, and He lives in the ever present.

One day, the world's throne will be occupied by Jesus Christ—King of the Jews, King of Israel, King of kings, King over all the earth, and King of glory. Remember, it is through the lens of biblical prophecy that we should view the conflicts of today and find our hope for tomorrow.

Things in this world are going to get better. They may get a little worse before they get better depending on how long the Savior waits. But we've got a great future ahead of us, and a little bit of the greatness of that future is in our heart to keep us hungry for when it will be the law of the land. What a thrill it is to know the King and to address Him in that way.

God has placed a throne in our heart. And of all the kingly titles of Jesus Christ, the one that is most personal to you and me is when we say, "Lord, You are my King. I vacate the throne of my heart Lord, and I give it to You. I want You to rule and reign in my life. Under my control I make too many mistakes and get into too many messes. Forgive me for ever thinking I could be my own monarch, that I could ever chart my own destiny."

The moment we receive Jesus Christ as Lord, a coronation takes place inside of us. Jesus becomes the King of our life, and we give Him the glory. Let Jesus Christ be your King.

APPLICATION

Personal Questions

1. Read Matthew 2:2, 27:11, and Mark 15:9–13, 26. In what two periods of His life was Jesus called by the title "King of the Jews"?

2. Read John 1:49, 12:13, and Matthew 27:42.

    a. Who was the first person in the Bible to recognize that Jesus was the King of Israel?

    b. List the other two times in Jesus' life when He was called by this title and who referred to Him this way.

3. Read Revelation 19:16. Out of all of Jesus' many titles, which is the ultimate title of royal honor?

4. Read Psalm 24:7, 10. What is Jesus' millennial title?

5. Explain the difference between having Jesus as your Savior and having Him as your King.

6. Read Isaiah 35:5–6. What four infirmities will be nonexistent during the coming Golden Age?

7. According to Zechariah 12:10 and 13:1, what will happen to the entire nation of Israel?

8. In Revelation 11:15, what happens at the end of the thousand-year reign of Jesus?

Group Questions

1. After reading Matthew 2:2, 27:11, and Mark 15:9–13, 26 as a group, you'll notice that the title "King of the Jews" was spoken with reverence at His birth. Discuss how this title was viewed differently at His death.

2. If comfortable, share with the group how Jesus came to be your Savior, and talk about the importance of making Him your King. What might that look like in a person's life?

3. Read Jeremiah 31:34 together. When Jesus sits on His throne again, will there be a need to teach others about Him? Why or why not?

4. After reading Isaiah 11:3–4 and Psalm 72:2, 4, 12, and 14, discuss how ethics will be different during the coming Golden Age.

5. Do you find world politics and elections concerning? Read Psalm 10:16 as a group and discuss how it feels to know that we don't have to worry about Jesus not having a successor.

D I D   Y O U   K N O W ?

Right now, kings are a scarce class. It is far more common today to have presidents and prime ministers lead the governments of nations rather than kings. Only forty-three monarchies are left on earth, most of which are ceremonial in nature. Since Elizabeth II passed away in 2022, the most famous royal figure in the world is her son King Charles III. A few other European nations still have royal families—Andorra, Belgium, Luxembourg, Spain, and Monaco. There are also some monarchies in the Muslim world, such as in Saudi Arabia, and a few exist in Asia. But nowadays, royal families are better known for their celebrity than for their sovereignty.

Notes
1. "Christmas Broadcast 2011," *Their Majesties' Work as Prince of Wales and Duchess of Cornwall*, November 17, 2015, https://www.royal.uk/christmas-broadcast-2011.
2. Quoted in "People," *Time*, April 17, 1978, https://content.time.com/time/subscriber/article/0,33009,916073-3,00.html.
3. J. Dwight Pentecost, *Things to Come: A Study in Biblical Eschatology* (Grand Rapids, MI: Zondervan, 1958).

LESSON 4

NO DEVIL

REVELATION 20:1–3

In this lesson we learn about our adversary, Satan, and about what he will be doing during the coming Golden Age.

Satan has been tempting mankind since the garden of Eden and continues to roam the earth like a lion, "seeking whom he may devour" (1 Peter 5:8). But during the coming Golden Age, he will not be active on the earth, and we will be freed from his tyranny. Studying the varied names used in Scripture for Satan gives us insight into who he is and how he acts.

OUTLINE

I. The Person of the Devil
    A. The Dragon
    B. The Serpent of Old
    C. The Devil
    D. Satan

II. The Prison of Demons

III. The Period of Deliverance

OVERVIEW

Sitting on thirty-seven acres of land southwest of Colorado Springs is a place called ADX Florence. It is the most secure prison in America. If you could walk its corridors, you'd pass a "who's who" of criminals, including Terry Nichols, who helped plan the 1995 Oklahoma City bombing; James Marcello, the notorious Chicago crime boss; El Chapo, the Mexican drug kingpin; and Dzhokhar Tsarnaev, the infamous Boston Marathon bomber, who is currently on death row. In fact, the criminals who go to that prison don't usually come out—they usually die there. The average prison sentence is twenty-two years, and each prisoner is kept in near-total solitary confinement with little or no time outside their cells.

The cells are 7 feet by 12 feet with a stool, desk, and bed made of poured concrete. The cells are soundproof with multiple cameras monitoring each prisoner twenty-four hours a day. Each cell has a small, narrow window designed so the prisoners do not know where they are in the complex.[1]

And here's the interesting thing: there has never been an escape from ADX Florence.

I only know of one other penitentiary more secure than that supermax. Designed by Almighty God for the worst of the evil agents in the universe, that prison is known as the "bottomless pit" or the "abyss."

According to Revelation 20, when Jesus comes back to set up His millennial kingdom and the Golden Age begins, an angel will come from heaven and bind Satan. John describes this event in verses 1–3:

> Then I saw an angel . . . having the key to the bottomless pit and a great chain in his hand. He laid hold of the dragon, that serpent of old, who is the Devil and Satan, and bound him for a thousand years; and he cast him into the bottomless pit, and shut him up, and set a seal on him, so that he should deceive the nations no more till the thousand years were finished.

Satan will be confined to the "bottomless pit" for the entirety of the coming Golden Age. The world will be free of Satan for 52,000 weeks—a thousand devil-less years!

There are three things to know about these opening verses in Revelation 20.

The Person of the Devil

First, we have the person of the devil. You will not find a phrase in the Bible with a more accurate description of the devil than this phrase: "the dragon, that serpent of old, who is the Devil and Satan" (Revelation 20:2).

Here there are four names—not of four different people, but four names for the same person. It is a list of names that carries a sense of authority like you were going to announce them before they were thrown into jail. And what's behind these four names is very interesting.

The Dragon

First of all, John refers to the devil as a dragon in Revelation 12. He sees a sign of a great, fiery red dragon who sought to kill the Messiah at the time of our Lord's first coming (see verses 1–5) and who will dominate the events around His second coming as well.

Here in Revelation 20, John identifies the ultimate version of the dragon. He says the dragon is Satan, the devil.

The Serpent of Old

Next, the Bible calls Satan the "serpent of old."

This takes us all the way back to Genesis 3, when the serpent appeared in the garden of Eden to tempt Eve and Adam into doubting and disobeying God. Satan deceives us by misquoting the Bible. He used that tactic on Eve in the garden, and he tried to use it on our Lord in the desert (see Matthew 4:1–11). Satan uses this subtle method of taking Scripture taken out of context to deceive many.

Satan usually does not deny the Scripture. Instead, he deceives by adding or subtracting his own words from Scripture. He takes Scripture out of context; he uses it the way it was never intended to be used. Sadly, Satan knows the Scripture better than most of us, and he's not afraid to twist its words. He hasn't changed any of his strategies. He keeps using them over and over and over.

The Devil

Then John gives us the third title for this evil person: "the dragon, that serpent of old, who is the Devil" (verse 2).

Our English word for "devil" comes from the Latin word *diabolus*, which means "one who accuses or slanders." The Bible tells us that the devil is our accuser. He comes before the Father, and he says something like this, "Did you see David Jeremiah down on earth this week, how he lost his cool, how he got upset, how he did this or that?" He slanders us; he tries to make us something before God that God does not accept. But we don't have to worry about the devil's accusations because we have our own advocate, Jesus Christ the Righteous, who is there making intercession for us.

Satan's purpose is to be a slanderer. Slander is gossip that involves the spreading of harmful information about someone in order to damage their character. Have we ever lived in such a slanderous context as we do now? Every time you turn around it's happening. This is exactly what the devil does. And behind all slander is the devil's influence.

In Genesis 3, the devil slandered God in front of Adam and Eve when he said, "God knows that in the day you eat of it your eyes will be opened, and you will be like God, knowing good and evil" (verse 5). Cunningly, the devil spun a tale about God with the intention of tarnishing His reputation and portraying the Lord as someone who is stingy instead of someone who is generous.

From that day until now, Satan has delighted in accusing God's children before the throne, pointing out our faults and making accusations against us. He did it with Job (see Job 1:9–11), he did it with Joshua the high priest (see Zechariah 3:1), and he did it with the entire family of believers (see Revelation 12:10–12). He is always at us, but he is running a futile scam because we're covered with the blood of Jesus. We're under the protection of Christ. Yet the devil keeps trying, even though he can't succeed.

Satan

The final name is his most famous title—he is Satan. "He laid hold of the dragon, that serpent of old, who is the Devil and Satan" (Revelation 20:2).

The term "Satan" comes straight from the Greek word *satanas*, which means "adversary." Satan is not your friend. He's not trying to help you get better; he's trying to destroy you. His ultimate goal is your death. He is your adversary.

The word *satanas* occurs more than thirty times in the New Testament. Satan tempts us (see 1 Corinthians 7:5); he takes advantage of us (see 2 Corinthians 2:11); he hinders us (see 1 Thessalonians 2:18). He provokes us to lie; he deceives us (see Acts 5:3); he tries to steal the Word of God from our hearts (see Mark 4:15).

If Satan gets his way, he will do what the Antichrist does at the very end of time when he sets himself up as God in the temple and demands that people worship him.

Where did Satan begin? He began with that very ploy. He wanted to be worshiped; he wanted to be God. He wanted God's worship to be directed to him.

Today, Satan continues his strategy of division. He injects the poison of suspicion and intolerance and hatred and jealousy. All of the ugliness we are witnessing today in the form of anti-Semitism on our campuses, in our churches, and in many of our schools isn't just something that happened. Anti-Semitism is from the pit of hell. It is satanic. The Bible says that those who bless Israel will be blessed and those who curse Israel will be cursed.

We now know who the devil is.

The Prison of Demons

Second, we discover the prison into which Satan is cast.

The Bible says, "Then I saw an angel coming down from heaven, having the key to the bottomless pit and a great chain in his hand. He laid hold of the dragon, that serpent of old, who is the Devil and Satan, and bound him for a thousand years; and he cast him into the bottomless pit, and shut him up" (Revelation 20:1–3).

The phrase "bottomless pit" means "a very deep place." This is God's supermax prison. And no one will ever escape from this prison either. For a thousand years, Satan will be banished from earth and imprisoned in this mysterious penitentiary. It isn't hell, for hell is the devil's final destination.

The book of Jude says, "And the angels who did not keep their positions of authority but abandoned their proper dwelling—these he has kept in darkness, bound with everlasting chains for judgment on the great Day" (verse 6 NIV).

When the angels followed Satan in his rebellion, many of them were cast into the abyss. Some of them are free and help Satan carry on his activities. For reasons only God knows, He's allowed the devil and some of his evil spirits to travel around earth's atmosphere. But He's imprisoned many of them.

In Luke 8, Jesus cast demons out of a man. When those demons came out, they repeatedly begged Jesus not to order them to go into the abyss. It was a place they dreaded. During the trumpet judgments of Revelation 9, an angel will open the shaft leading to the abyss and release these malignant and heinous demons, and during the Tribulation they will be set free. One of the reasons the Tribulation will be such an awful time is that demonic activity will be at an all-time high. The demons of hell will be released to bring along with them the judgment and hate and death that's a part of that seven-year period.

John tells us in Revelation 20 that the devil will be bound with chains he cannot escape, that he will be consigned to a prison he cannot avoid, and that he will be there for every single day of the Millennium. That's why it's called the Golden Age—there will be no devil!

The Period of Deliverance

Third, John mentions the period of deliverance.

During this time, John said Satan will "deceive the nations no more till the thousand years [are] finished" (Revelation 20:3). During the millennial reign of Christ, the Golden Age, we who live and govern with Christ on earth will be delivered from Satan's tyranny.

Swiss theologian René Pache wrote, "What change shall take place when the tempter is no longer able to seduce the nations! That will be better than it was in Eden, for in Eden, Satan was allowed to tempt our first parents."[2]

Nothing like that could ever happen in the Millennium. This doesn't mean there won't be sin on earth. Those with mortal bodies will still battle their fallen nature, and the blessed eternal state of the new heaven and new earth are yet to come. But think of this: Today you and I have three enemies as Christians. Those enemies are the world, the flesh, and the devil. Consider how different it will be when one of those three is gone and we will not be bedeviled by our enemy.

Paul said the devil is "the god of this age" (2 Corinthians 4:4). And during the coming Golden Age, he will lose his power.

Gone will be his ability to amplify sexual temptation and marital infidelity (see 1 Corinthians 7:5). While we may be tempted, we will not have to confront the enticements of Satan (see Matthew 4:1–11). We'll not have to contend with being sifted as wheat by his evil designs (see Luke 22:31). Nor will he fill our hearts to lie to one another as he did with Ananias in Acts 5. We'll be able to forgive one another because we'll be free from Satan's devices (see 2 Corinthians 2:11).

He will not swoop down on us in unexpecting moments and snatch the Word out of our hearts while we're walking out of church on Sunday. He won't hinder the workers of God as he did in 1 Thessalonians 2. He will be physically and spiritually bound in that prison and then will be in hell forever.

Gone will be Satan's ability to plague us with demonically caused natural disasters. We'll be freed from his ability to hinder the work of the Lord on this planet. No longer will he create agitation among the nations. Again, the Bible says that in the age that is to come, we will study war no more (see Isaiah 2:4). War will be ended; Satan won't be causing wars. He will be unable to trouble the nations, for he will be consigned to the bottomless pit.

The Bible tells us that Satan was "a murderer from the beginning" (John 8:44). When he's gone, we should expect that murder will be virtually nonexistent during the Golden Age. He "has sinned from the beginning" (1 John 3:8), so we would expect for people in the Golden Age to be a little more righteous and exhibit character that we haven't seen in a long time. Satan is "puffed up with pride" (1 Timothy 3:6). When he's gone, we might be more humble than we are right now.

Today, the devil makes many people take leave of their senses and do his will (see 2 Timothy 2:26). The coming Golden Age will be a time of wisdom and sensibility. The devil delights in throwing God's children into prison and persecuting them in all manner of ways (see Revelation 2:10). Satan is active in our world, and he can do things that you wouldn't imagine he could do. Satanism is on the rise today. *Newsweek* magazine published a major article titled, "Satan Is Getting Hot as Hell in American Pop Culture." The writer, who covers cultural trends for *Newsweek,* wrote, "The Devil is front and center in movies, TV shows, podcasts and even children's books.... On Netflix alone there are dozens of titles dealing with hellish demons."[3]

Attendance in our churches is waning. Spirituality is not moving forward. The void that's been created by the lack of Christianity moving in the right direction is being filled with some of these satanic things. If you watch carefully, you will notice it. If you look around when you're traveling, there are satanist churches, and they advertise in front of their churches that they are a satanist church. There are all kinds of internet sites for satanism, and interestingly enough, some very famous people have become followers of Satan.

As frightening as that is, remember we may be only seven years from the moment when God will throw Satan into the abyss and slam the door on him. And the knowledge of that future should comfort us today.

We shouldn't become overly conscious of the devil, but we shouldn't ever let him get out of our sight. We don't believe Satan's defeat is just a future event. He's already defeated and is just waiting for his sentence to be carried out. In the meantime, he's very active. Why is he active? Because he knows his time is short. His judgment is coming. Satan has been defeated, but he's not yet banished and consigned to the abyss.

So stay alert and watch out for your great enemy the devil, for he prowls around like a roaring lion seeking someone to devour (see 1 Peter 5:8). Satan wants to devour you. He wants to devour me. He most of all wants to devour your influence and take you out of the game so that you can't be an active participant anymore. And he is doing this over and over and over again, almost on a weekly basis.

We also need to stay confident in the Lord. Remember, the Bible says, "Greater is he that is in you, than he that is in the world" (1 John 4:4 KJV). In other words, the One who lives within you is greater than Satan.

Randy Alcorn writes, "What's the opposite of light? Darkness. What's the opposite of good? Evil. When asked to name the opposite of God, people often answer, 'Satan.' But that's false. Michael, the righteous archangel, is Satan's opposite. Satan is finite; God is infinite. God has no equal."[4]

Satan isn't even in God's universe. He doesn't belong in the same sentence with God. He is no match for God. God is overwhelmingly greater than Satan. Satan may be powerful, but his power is nothing. And when God deems it necessary for him to be gone, he'll be gone for a thousand years. And then when the thousand years are over, he'll be cast into the lake of fire, and his doom will be final.

I remember reading years ago about a book called *Your God Is Too Small*. And one writer said that another book should be written titled *Your Devil Is Too Big.*[5] Because while we're to watch out for him, he's no threat to our salvation. He's no threat to our God. When we put the devil in his place, put on the whole armor of God, and stand our ground, we have nothing to worry about.

Steve Brown tells a story from his childhood about being troubled by a bully in his neighborhood. One day the bully entered his yard, and he was terrified. After a few tense moments he decided he'd had enough of this, and he decided to confront the bully head-on. So he bravely walked toward him, and to his surprise the bully seemed scared and began trembling. Steve felt empowered and thought to himself, *Man, I'm really something!* Then he turned around and saw his father standing on the porch behind him.[6]

When Satan comes, your heavenly Father is standing on the porch behind you. You don't fight Satan alone. You have the Father, the Son, the Holy Spirit, and this promise from His Word: "No temptation has overtaken you except such as is common to man; but God is faithful, who will not allow you to be tempted beyond what you are able, but with the temptation will also make the way of escape, that you may be able to bear it" (1 Corinthians 10:13).

You don't have to be afraid of Satan. But you do have to be aware of him; you have to be knowledgeable about him.

Satan is nothing but a counterfeiter. Jesus is the Light of the World; Satan wants to be an angel of light. Jesus is the King of kings; Satan is king over the children of pride. Jesus is the Prince of Peace; Satan is the prince of the world, the prince of the power of the air. Jesus is the Lord our God; Satan is the god of this age. Jesus is the Lion of the Tribe of Judah; Satan is a roaring lion, going about seeking whom he may devour.

Satan just keeps coming back with the same testing of the lust of the flesh, the lust of the eyes, and the pride of life. It's what he did to Adam and Eve, it's what he did to Jesus in the desert, and it's the way that he's coming after us.

The Bible says we're not to be ignorant of Satan's strategies. We're to be alert, to stand against him, to put on the whole armor of God, and to use the Word of God to defeat him. Don't be afraid. The God you serve is the Creator of the universe. He can handle Satan.

APPLICATION

Personal Questions

1. Read Revelation 20:1–3. List and describe the four names of the devil that are found in this passage.

2. Read Revelation 12:1–5. In these verses, how did John describe Satan?

3. Read Genesis 3:1–6.

   a. How did the serpent tempt Eve in the garden of Eden?

   b. In what ways does Satan use the same strategy today?

4. What are some examples from Scripture of Satan slandering people before God?

5. Why are Satan's accusations against us as Christians unsuccessful?

6. Read 1 Corinthians 7:5, 2 Corinthians 2:11, and Acts 5:3.

   a. What are the actions Satan takes in each of these verses?

   b. What do these verses teach us about how Satan attacks Christians?

7. According to Revelation 20:3, where will Satan be during the coming Golden Age?

8. Describe what we won't have to face in the Millennium because Satan will be bound.

9. How does 1 John 4:4 give you strength as you face temptation and observe what is happening in today's culture?

10. In what way(s) can you be more alert of Satan's strategies and be more prepared to stand against him?

Group Questions

1. Read Revelation 20:1–3 as a group and discuss the four names of Satan mentioned in these verses.

2. Read Matthew 4:1–11 together.

   a. How did Satan use Scripture to try to deceive Jesus?

   b. How did Jesus respond to Satan after each temptation?

   c. What lesson can we learn from Christ about battling temptation?

3. Describe how Satan slanders Christians before God. Why are his attempts to slander us always unsuccessful?

4. As a group, read Job 1:9–11. What accusations did Satan make before God about Job?

5. Read each of the following verses and list the action Satan takes in each one.

   a. 1 Corinthians 7:5

   b. 2 Corinthians 2:11

   c. 1 Thessalonians 2:18

   d. Acts 5:3

   e. Mark 4:15

6. What does Revelation 20:2–3 tell us about where Satan will spend the Millennium?

7. Discuss the section "The Period of Deliverance."

   a. In what ways do you think life on earth will be different with Satan bound?

   b. How does this make you anticipate the coming Golden Age?

8. Read 1 John 4:4 and 1 Corinthians 10:13 together.

   a. What do these verses teach us about God and our ability to resist temptation?

   b. How can you remember the truths of these verses and put them into practice when you are tempted?

DID YOU KNOW?

There are more than 3,000 different types of snakes found throughout the world, and in early 2024 scientists discovered a new—and now the largest— snake species: a green anaconda in the rainforest of Ecuador.[7] The majority of people will never encounter a green anaconda, but all of us as Christians will be tempted by "the serpent of old" (Revelation 20:2). Thankfully, we are equipped with the armor of God so that we can be victorious in spiritual warfare. But we must heed Paul's words to "be strong in the Lord and in the power of His might. Put on the whole armor of God, that you may be able to stand against the wiles of the devil" (Ephesians 6:10–11).

Notes
1. "The World's Most Secure Buildings: ADX Florence Prison," *IDENTIV*, July 20, 2022, https:// www.identiv.com/resources/blog/the-worlds-most-secure-buildings-adx-florence-prison.
2. René Pache, *The Return of Jesus Christ* (Chicago, IL: Moody, 1955), 395.
3. Paul Bond, "Satan Is Getting Hot as Hell in American Pop Culture," *Newsweek*, March 28, 2023, https://www.newsweek.com/satan-getting-hot-hell-american-pop-culture-1790669.
4. Randy Alcorn, *If God Is Good: Faith in the Midst of Suffering and Evil* (Colorado Springs, CO: Multnomah Books, 2009), 51.
5. Erwin Lutzer, *God's Devil* (Chicago, IL: Moody Publishers, 2015), 23.
6. Steve Brown, "Satan Is Real & Out to Get You," *Key Life*, June 14, 2023, https://www.keylife.org/ articles/steves-devotional-satan-is-real-out-to-get-you/.
7. "New Species of Amazon Anaconda, World's Largest Snake, Discovered," *Reuters*, March 1, 2024, https://www.reuters.com/world/americas/ new-species-amazon-anaconda-worlds-largest-snake-discovered-2024-03-01/.

OLD AGE IN THE GOLDEN AGE

ISAIAH 65:20

*In this lesson we learn about the longevity of life throughout
history and during the Millennium.*

In Genesis, we read of Adam, Lamech, Noah, and others who lived for
centuries. Thousands of years later, the average lifespan is measured
in decades, not centuries. But in the coming Golden Age, those who live
through the Tribulation and enter the Millennium will once again experience long life. Reading about Jesus' authority over sin and sickness, and
learning about Scriptures containing proverbs that guide us in how to live
a long life, give us hope.

OUTLINE

I. **The Reduction of Longevity**

II. **The Restoration of Longevity**

III. **The Redemption of Longevity**

OVERVIEW

They call her "Super Grandmother." As of this writing, she's 117 years old and the oldest living woman in the world. Maria Branyas was born in San Francisco back in March of 1907. When her father's health declined in 1915, her family moved back to their hometown of Catalonia, Spain, where Maria has remained for more than a century.

Incredibly, Maria doesn't get sick. In her words, "I have not suffered from any illness or been through an operating room." She has no trace of cardiovascular disease commonly found in elderly people, nor has she suffered any memory loss or decline in cognitive function. In fact, she can vividly recount memories from when she was four years old. Aside from some slight hearing loss and mobility issues, she's in wonderful health.

Maria credits her own longevity to a simple life and the daily consumption of natural yogurt. More specifically, she has benefited from "order, tranquility, good connection with family and friends, contact with nature, emotional stability, lots of positivity and [staying] away from toxic people."

As you might expect, a lot of people have taken notice of Maria's incredible combination of longevity and vitality. That includes world-renowned geneticist and researcher Dr. Manel Esteller, who is leading a study to analyze "six billion segments of Maria's DNA, focusing on 200 genes" connected with the aging process. His goal is to develop treatments that can address degenerative diseases in our neurological and cardiovascular systems associated with old age.[1]

I hope Dr. Esteller and his researchers are successful at improving the aging process for all people, myself included, but I'm afraid the best we can hope for right now is improvement. No matter whom we study or what treatments we develop, our lives on this earth will continue to be measured in decades, not centuries.

But what about the ages to come? Is it reasonable for us to hope that lifespans will increase in Christ's millennial kingdom?

Yes! It's more than reasonable, and we can more than hope. We can believe in the historical testimony of God's Word, we can rely on the incredible authority demonstrated by Jesus during His earthly ministry, and we can accept in faith the inspiring promises God has already given us for that glorious Golden Age.

There will be two groups of people who will go into the Millennium, the thousand-year period after the Tribulation. Those of us who have been raptured or resurrected will be there with Jesus. If you're a Christian, you'll be in the Millennium. When Jesus comes back at the end of the Tribulation, we come back with Him, and we go right into the Millennium. We who are the raised or raptured will never die again. We'll dwell with Him for a thousand years, and then we'll make a transition into the new heaven and the new earth, where we'll be with Him forever. No more death for us! Nor sickness or sin! No more pain, no pining away. Once you get into eternity and you go to heaven, that's all history. And when you get to the Millennium, you will live for one thousand years in the Golden Age and then go to heaven!

The other group who goes into the Millennium are those who were saved during the Tribulation, or survived the Tribulation, and the people who will be born to those families in the Tribulation. These people will experience the kind of longevity reminiscent of the early days of Genesis.

That's the focus of this lesson. Some of these Tribulation survivors will die during the Millennium, but death will be very rare, and people's lifespans will extend for centuries.

The Reduction of Longevity

When God created the human race, He had eternity in mind. Death was not part of God's original creation. Death is a result of sin. Death is the result of disobedience. But God has placed eternity in our hearts (see Ecclesiastes 3:11), and even after the Fall, after Adam and Eve sinned, humans lived for vast periods of time.

The oldest man in the Genesis record is Methuselah, who lived to the ripe old age of 969—almost a full millennium (see Genesis 5:27). But he wasn't the only example of long life. He wasn't even an outlier.

- Adam lived for 930 years (see Genesis 5:5).
- Seth lived for 912 years (see Genesis 5:8).

- Jared, Adam's great-great-great grandson, lived to be 962 (see Genesis 5:20).
- Lamech, the father of Noah, was 777 when he passed away (see Genesis 5:31).
- Noah, who was 600 years old when God flooded the earth, lived for 350 years after the Flood and died at 950 years of age (see Genesis 9:29).

So, what are we to make of these numbers? Are these exaggerations intended to show the stature of these great people? Are they the result of mishaps in the translation of the Bible? I don't think any of these explanations are true. When it comes to Scripture, it's always been my firm belief that we should take God at His word. In this case, Genesis presents these extended ages as historical information, and we should accept them as such.

We don't know for sure why people lived for centuries, but here are some possible explanations. Perhaps the climate of the earth was so much different in those early days that it allowed for increased longevity. Many scholars believe there was a vapor barrier or a canopy around the earth that made our atmosphere more conducive to long life, something akin to the ozone layer. It's possible this canopy collapsed or dissipated during the Flood. Maybe the genetic pool was so young that people were more vigorous. Or perhaps the grace of God was so fresh that His children lived for many centuries.

What the book of Genesis does make clear is that something happened after Noah's flood. Not only was the physical structure of our planet altered in major ways, but the span of human lives also decreased significantly. For instance, Shem, one of Noah's sons, lived for 600 years (see 11:10–11). But Shem's grandson Salah lived for 433 years (see 11:14–15). Terah, who was Abraham's father, lived for 205 years before he died in Haran (see 11:32).

In Genesis 6:3, God adjusted the human lifespan: "My Spirit shall not strive with man forever, for he is indeed flesh; yet his days shall be one hundred and twenty years."

The patriarch Jacob may have been referring to this when he told Pharoah, "The days of the years of my pilgrimage are one hundred and thirty years; few and evil have been the days of the years of my life, and they have not attained to the days of the years of the life of my fathers" (Genesis 47:9). In other words, "I'm not nearly as old as my mom and dad or my grandpa and grandma."

The cycles of life continued to decline until Moses declared in Psalm 90:10, "The days of our lives are seventy years; and if by reason of strength they are eighty years, yet their boast is only labor and sorrow; for it is soon cut off, and we fly away."

From long lives of centuries, to shortened lives of approximately 120 years, to seventy and eighty years. That's the progression of God's providence over the lifespan of people on earth. From old age at the beginning, through shortened life in the here and now, to the ultimate long life in the Millennium.

Perhaps it is the mercy and grace of God that reduces the amount of time we spend in this vale of tears we call the earth. I've said this before—life is hard, and this world is a war zone for the soul. The book of Job says, "Man is born to trouble, as the sparks fly upward" (5:7). And the apostle Paul longed to depart and be with Christ, "which," he said, "is far better" (Philippians 1:23).

Isaiah 57:1 is a fascinating verse. It says, "Good people pass away; the godly often die before their time. But no one seems to care or wonder why. No one seems to understand that God is protecting them from the evil to come" (NLT). The Bible says sometimes death comes to protect us from the evil that is to come.

The Restoration of Longevity

First, life was reduced, but in the coming Golden Age there will be a restoration of longevity.

Praise the Lord! Things will be different in the Millennium. Here's some reasons why that's going to be true. The devil will be bound. The earth will again become the healthiest environment we could imagine for human life. God will extend the lifespans of the men and women who come out of the Tribulation and who produce children. People's lifespans will be extended again as they were in the early days of Genesis so they can enjoy the good to come.

Christ will be at the center of the millennial kingdom, ruling on the throne of His ancestor David in Jerusalem. His power and authority will radiate throughout that kingdom for the benefit of all who are citizens. On a spiritual level, that means the Lamb of God will repair the effects of sin and Satan in our world. He will restore what was lost and reclaim everything that was taken away in the original curse, and His intent for creation will be restored.

On a practical level, that means our physical bodies will no longer reflect the consequences of sin. We won't deal with the kinds of physical problems that the world faces now.

Jesus gave us a preview of His power and authority while He was on this earth more than 2,000 years ago. There were many moments when His kingly nature broke through and He asserted His authority over sin and sickness.

One such example is found in Luke 5. "And it happened when He was in a certain city, that behold, a man who was full of leprosy saw Jesus; and he fell on his face and implored Him, saying, 'Lord, if You are willing, You can make me clean'" (verse 12).

Now, leprosy was the most feared of all the afflictions in ancient times. There was no cure, and lepers died slowly from the escalating degradation of their bodies. Worse still, they were not allowed to be a part of the Jewish community. They were considered cursed. They were segregated and isolated, living in leper colonies.

Can you hear the pain in this man's words when he begged Jesus for healing? He said, "Can You make me clean?" Jesus responded not as the sacrificial Lamb of God but as the now-and-future King. "He put out His hand and touched him, saying, 'I am willing; be cleansed.' Immediately the leprosy left him" (Luke 5:13).

In the Millennium, Christ will do for everyone what He did for the leper in the Gospels. He will remove all sickness, all deformities, and all handicaps. In the coming Golden Age, His reign will be over a world where there is no blindness, no deafness, and no muteness. No eyeglasses, no hearing aids, no speech therapy, no wheelchairs, no crutches, and no walkers.

We have these promises. And, as we have learned, so much of the information about this period of time is found in the Old Testament Scriptures. Isaiah 29:18 says, "In that day the deaf shall hear the words of the book, and the eyes of the blind shall see out of obscurity and out of darkness." Isaiah 35:5–6 says, "Then the eyes of the blind shall be opened, and the ears of the deaf shall be unstopped. Then the lame shall leap like a deer, and the tongue of the dumb sing." And Jeremiah 30:17 says, "I will restore health to you and heal you of your wounds."

During the thousand-year reign of Christ, sickness and death will not exist among the resurrected saints, and death will be a very rare occurrence among the survivors of the Tribulation.

The Redemption of Longevity

Next, we come to the redemption of longevity.

Despite the best efforts of our medical experts, there is little chance that any of us will become another Methuselah. But all that will change during the Millennium. In that age, human longevity will return to pre-Flood levels. Even better, the lives of the redeemed who rule this world with Christ will return to pre-Eden levels.

We will once again live forever!

It is as though history will come full circle. The quantity and quality of our years will once again reveal the goodness of our Creator and reflect His infallible design.

This is how Isaiah describes it: "Never again will there be in it an infant who lives but a few days, or an old man who does not live out his years; the one who dies at a hundred will be thought a mere child; the one who fails to reach a hundred will be considered accursed" (65:20 NIV).

Not only will people live much longer, but there will also be a tremendous increase in the birthrate as children are born to those who survive the Tribulation. Jeremiah 30:19–20 says, "I will multiply them, and they shall not diminish; I will also glorify them, and they shall not be small. Their children also shall be as before, and their congregation shall be established before Me."

Scholar Alva J. McClain says, "Disease will be abolished. . . . The crisis of death will be experienced only by those incorrigible individuals who rebel against the laws of [the] kingdom. The ordinary hazards of physical life will be under the direct control of the voice of the One who said, 'Peace be still,' to the winds and the waves."[2]

The Millennium is when we will begin to experience our true destiny—our true design. Through the power of our Lord Jesus Christ and under the authority of His reign, our lives will stretch into the centuries with only the promise of paradise on the horizon.

But the question is, What do we do until then? Someone told me some years ago that there are three options that we have as humans: we can wear out, we can rust out, or we can live out.

Some folks wear out. And if we're not careful, that's what life will do to us. It is possible to wear out the human body before its time.

Some people rust out. They just don't do anything, and they're like an old car that's left out with no protection. They just rust out and vanish.

And then there's some people who live out. This is God's plan for us: to treasure this life He has given us. It might not last a thousand years, but life is good. And we should take every day as a gift from Him and be thankful for it. We should be good stewards of life the best we know how, work hard to correct all the issues we face, never give up, and never say, "Okay that's it, I quit." We should do everything we can to live every day for the glory of God and live as long as we can, knowing that when life is over, it gets even better. That's the attitude we should have.

Now, the Bible doesn't promise us a thousand years. But there are more than twenty places in the Bible that say, in essence, "If you do this, you'll live a long life." These passages are found primarily in the books of Proverbs and Psalms. We need to remember that they are proverbs, not promises. The book of Proverbs is made up of the wise sayings of Solomon, and they are the sayings about life as it normally is.

Here's an illustration. Many of you, if you have trouble with your children, will be directed to a verse in the Bible that says, "Train up a child in the way he should go, and when he is old he will not depart from it" (Proverbs 22:6). And then you do what that says, and it doesn't happen. It seems as if the book of Proverbs made you a promise, and the promise wasn't kept.

But the book of Proverbs didn't actually *make* you a promise. It just said this is what *normally* happens. There are promises, and there are proverbs. And these statements about long life are proverbs. They give you clues about the quality of your life. So, just like you can go to a seminar and learn about how to do things to help your physical life, these verses are a short little seminar on how to live your life and the character traits that God will honor in your life.

In the rest of this lesson, we will cover ten of the twenty proverbs about what we can do to experience a long life.

Number 1: Keep God's commandments. 1 Kings 3:14 says, "If you walk in My ways, to keep My statutes and My commandments . . . I will lengthen your days."

Number 2: Tell the truth. There are three "long-life" principles packed into three verses in Psalm 34, and the first is to tell the truth. "Does anyone want to live a life that is long and prosperous? Then keep your tongue from speaking evil and your lips from telling lies!" (verses 12–13 NLT). People who tell lies run the risk of not living as long as they could.

Number 3: Turn from evil. "Does anyone want to live a life that is long and prosperous? . . . Turn away from evil and do good" (Psalm 34:12, 14 NLT).

Number 4: Search for peace. "Does anyone want to live a life that is long and prosperous? . . . Search for peace, and work to maintain it" (Psalm 34:12, 14 NLT). Don't be a troublemaker; be a peacemaker.

Number 5: Love the Lord. Psalm 91 says, "Because he has set his love upon Me, therefore I will deliver him. . . . With long life I will satisfy him" (verses 14, 16). When you love God, He wants to help you live for a long time. You might ask, "How do I know if I love God?" Here's the answer to that question: Are you serving Him? Because you love God by serving God.

Number 6: Treasure God's wisdom. Proverbs 3:16 says, "Length of days is in [wisdom's] right hand, in her left hand riches and honor." And Proverbs 4:10 says, "Hear, my son, and receive my sayings, and the years of your life will be many." Proverbs helps you to understand how to deal with people. So if you're reading Proverbs every day, month after month, you are being taught wisdom. And the Bible says that if you treasure God's wisdom, the years of your life will be many.

Number 7: Fear the Lord. "The fear of the LORD prolongs days" (Proverbs 10:27). Many people say, "The fear of the Lord is not being afraid of the Lord; it's being in awe of the Lord." That is true, but it also means being afraid of the Lord. There needs to be someone in your life of whom you are afraid, in a good sense. God wants us to fear Him in awe and worship but also to know He's not someone to be messed with.

Number 8: Control your tongue. "Those who control their tongue will have a long life; opening your mouth can ruin everything" (Proverbs 13:3 NLT). Scripture says that if you control your tongue, you have a chance at a long life. But if you keep opening your mouth in the wrong way, it will ruin everything.

Number 9: Cultivate true humility. Proverbs 22:4 says, "True humility and fear of the LORD lead to riches, honor, and long life" (NLT). Humility is often misunderstood, but the Bible has a lot to say about it. One of the simplest ways to explain it is that humility is not thinking less about yourself, it's just thinking about yourself less. The Bible says that if we don't humble ourselves, God will humble us. And Proverbs 27:2 says, "Let another man praise you, and not your own mouth."

Number 10: Honor your parents. That's the most famous one on the list. "'Honor your father and mother,' which is the first commandment with promise: 'that it may be well with you and you may live long on the earth'" (Ephesians 6:2–3). This is not just about when you're growing up under their leadership. It applies even after you get married. Honor your parents. Love your parents. Sometimes that's hard, but the Bible honors those who honor their parents.

I've found four things that are important to do as you go through life: be holy, be healthy, be humble, and be hungry. Live a holy life, emulating and worshiping God. Live a healthy life, taking responsibility for your health. Live a humble life, thinking more about others than yourself. Live a hungry life, learning something new every day. Never be comfortable thinking that you have arrived, because you haven't. God has so much more for us to learn and so many more areas for us to grow in throughout our life.

The World Health Organization reported that the global leading cause of death is heart disease, followed by strokes, lower respiratory infections, neonatal conditions, and Alzheimer's.[3] There are all kinds of causes of death that are reported, but the real cause of death is sin. The Bible says, "The soul who sins shall die" (Ezekiel 18:20). And Romans 6:23 says, "The wages of sin is death."

Only the Great Physician can give us everlasting healing of body, mind, and soul. And you cannot know the blessing of the Millennium unless you deal with your sin. The way you get to be a forever person is to ask Jesus

Christ into your heart, tell Him you're sorry for your sin, and say to Him that you want to be a Christian. When you become a Christian, you get all the benefits of who a Christian is—all the things that have been covered in this lesson—and then eternity in heaven on top of it all.

APPLICATION

Personal Questions

1. Read Genesis 5 and note how old each person was when he died.

    a. Adam

    b. Seth

    c. Enosh

    d. Cainan

    e. Mahalalel

    f. Jared

g. Methuselah

h. Lamech

2. What are some of the possible reasons why lifespans shortened after the Flood?

3. Read Isaiah 57:1. According to this verse, what does death protect the godly from?

4. Read Luke 5:12–14.

   a. What did the leper ask Jesus?

   b. What was Jesus' response to the leper?

   c. How does Jesus' healing of the leper give us insight into His role in relation to illness in the Millennium?

5. Read Isaiah 65:20. What does this verse teach us about longevity in the coming Golden Age?

6. Read Jeremiah 30:19–20 and explain what this verse teaches us about the birthrate during the Millennium.

7. Based on this lesson, what does it mean to rust out, wear out, or live out in life?

8. Choose five of the proverbs about a long life mentioned in this lesson and explain them below.

a. Which one of these is the hardest for you to do?

b. What is one action you can take this week to grow in that area?

Group Questions

1. Who are the two groups that will enter the Millennium? What will be unique about the lifespans of each group?

2. Read Genesis 5 together and discuss the long lives of those mentioned in the chapter. Why might people have lived for centuries at that time?

3. As a group, read Genesis 11:10–15, 32.

    a. How long are the lifespans found in this chapter of Genesis?

    b. According to Psalm 90:10, what did Moses say was the average length of life?

    c. Why was there a change in the length of time people lived (see Genesis 6:3)?

4. Read Isaiah 29:18, 35:5–6, and Jeremiah 30:17 together. Discuss what the restoration of longevity will be like in the Millennium for those who live through the Tribulation and for those born in the Millennium.

5. In this lesson, ten proverbs from Scripture about living a long life are mentioned. List and explain each of the proverbs.

6. If comfortable, share with the group which of the proverbs is most challenging for you and how you are planning to grow in that area.

7. Discuss the importance of being holy, healthy, humble, and hungry. How can you encourage each other to continue to learn and grow no matter your age?

DID YOU KNOW?

Bryan Johnson is a tech multimillionaire who has spent more than $4 million developing a life-extension system. In order to prevent his own death, Johnson goes through a rigorous daily routine that includes taking more than one hundred pills, monitoring his sleep, avoiding all unhealthy foods, applying eyedrops to prevent cataracts, exercising, and much more. "I don't think there's been any time in history where Homo sapiens could say with a straight face that death may not be inevitable," says Johnson. "Until now." [4] Of course, we know that no human being alive today can prevent death.

Notes

1. Jessica Baker, "GOLDEN AGE—I'm the Oldest Woman in the World but I Have NO Health Problems . . . Now Scientists Think I May Hold the Key to Immortality," *The U.S. Sun*, October 24, 2023, https://www.the-sun.com/health/9402264/oldest-woman-world-maria-branyas-key-immortality-spain/.
2. Adapted from unpublished notes by Alva J. McClain (Winona Lake, IN: Grace Seminary, n.d.), 7.
3. "The Top 10 Causes of Death," *World Health Organization*, December 9, 2020, https://www.who.int/news-room/fact-sheets/detail/the-top-10-causes-of-death.
4. Charlotte Alter, "The Man Who Thinks He Can Live Forever," *Time*, September 20, 2023, https://time.com/6315607/bryan-johnsons-quest-for-immortality/.

LESSON 6

THE END OF WAR

MICAH 4:3

In this lesson we learn about the peace we will experience on earth during the Millennium.

Throughout history, countries have gone to war with each other and people have opposed war, calling in vain for peace. But during Jesus' millennial reign, the earth will not be plagued with war as it has been for thousands of years. Instead, the coming Golden Age will be a thousand-year time of peace—a time when people and nations will no longer be at war with each other. As we read of the coming kingdom of peace, we can enjoy peace in our heart when we put Jesus in control of our life.

OUTLINE

I. **A World of War**

II. **A Kingdom of Peace**
   A. Peace from God
   B. Peace Among Nations

C. Peace in Nature
D. Peace Throughout Israel
E. Peace Between Enemies

OVERVIEW

Vladimir Putin called it a "special military operation." The rest of the world called it the largest ground invasion in Europe since World War II. In the early hours of February 24, 2022, explosions erupted across Ukraine, including the cities of Odessa, Kharkiv, Mariupol, and Kyiv. Russian airborne forces descended by the thousands, quickly amassing at the Hostomel Airport. And ground forces also poured into Ukraine by the hundreds of thousands from Russia and Belarus.

Speaking on Russian national television, Putin offered many justifications for his "operation," and he warned other nations to stay out of it. If they didn't, there would be "consequences [like they] have never seen."[1]

Looking back on it now, we have seen the awful nature of war. The first eighteen months of full-scale war between Russia and Ukraine resulted in nearly half a million soldiers wounded or killed on both sides.[2] According to the United Nations Refugee Agency, more than three million civilians have been displaced in Ukraine, with more than six million more refugees forced to flee into neighboring nations across Europe and around the globe. Almost fifteen million Ukrainians require humanitarian assistance, including those without proper access to food.[3]

Russian civilians have fared just about as badly as the Ukrainians. Many people think this has impacted just Ukraine and their soldiers. But the Russian economy has been jolted, many of their soldiers have been killed, and husbands and fathers are no longer coming home to their families. These are the consequences; these are the terrible realities of war.

Sometimes people ask me, "Do you think we'll ever have peace? Will there ever be a time of peace in this world?"

A study that's been done found that over the last 3,400 years, there have been 268 years of peace. Meaning, for more than 92% of human history, we have been forced to endure the specter of war.[4]

In more recent history, things have become even worse. Even a "peaceful" nation like the United States has endured two world wars, the Cold War, the Korean War, the Vietnam War, two wars involving Iraq, the war in Afghanistan, the war on terror, and the wars going on right now all over the world.

And people ask, "Why do we have to have war? What causes war?" The answer to that question is so very clearly presented in the book of James. James 4:1–2 says, "Where do wars and fights come from among you? Do they not come from your desires for pleasure that war in your members? You lust and do not have. You murder and covet and cannot obtain. You fight and war."

The Bible says war comes from our heart. The fallen heart of humanity explains why we fail at peace. But will that always be true?

A World of War

During World War I, C. S. Lewis was sent to the front lines of France. It was 1917. After a few weeks, he was hospitalized with a bout of trench fever. And when he was discharged from the hospital, he immediately returned to the front lines, where some months later he was wounded in three places by an exploding shell that killed the sergeant who was standing next to him when it exploded.

Not surprisingly, Lewis carried those experiences with him for the rest of his life. When World War II arrived, he wrote these words:

> My memories of the last war haunted my dreams for years. Military service, to be plain, includes the threat of every temporal evil: pain and death which is what we fear from sickness: isolation from those we love which is what we fear from exile: toil under arbitrary masters, injustice and humiliation, which is what we fear from slavery: hunger, thirst, cold and exposure which is what we fear from poverty. I'm not a pacifist. If it's got to be, it's got to be. But the flesh is weak and selfish and I think death would be much better than to live through another war.[5]

Most of us feel the way C. S. Lewis did. We feel like war is an interruption of life. Is war always harmful? Of course it is. Is it destructive?

Absolutely. Does war always involve a cost that feels too heavy to bear? It certainly does. But is war always wrong? No.

There are many, many reasons why war can be necessary. They're all sad. But they're necessary. There's a lot in the Bible about war. I wrote a paper some years ago called, "Is War Ever in the Will of God?" And I was really shocked to find out how much the Bible has to say about war.

Moses obeyed God's command to attack pagan kings and leaders. Deuteronomy 3:3–4 says, "So the LORD our God also delivered into our hands Og king of Bashan, with all his people, and we attacked him until he had no survivors remaining. And we took all his cities at that time; there was not a city which we did not take from them."

Joshua was the great military leader of the Old Testament, and he stood on the shores of Canaan with the command from God to go in and conquer Canaan. God gave him very specific instructions. He said, in essence, "Take out all of the survivors, don't leave any of the survivors in the Canaanite camps." The Canaanites were very wicked people, and God was not about to take a chance on their wickedness penetrating the Jewish bloodline and changing His purpose for them.

In the book of Joshua, we find that the soldiers didn't do what God told them to do. "The children of Judah could not drive [the Jebusites] out. . . . They put the Canaanites to forced labor, but did not utterly drive them out" (Joshua 15:63; 17:13). For the rest of their lives the people the Israelites didn't drive out were a nemesis to them. They were the ones who got in their way; they were the ones who drove them crazy. If they had done what God had told them to do, they wouldn't have had all that anguish. But they didn't.

The book of Revelation describes the moment at the end of the Tribulation when Jesus comes back as the Great Warrior. He leads the armies of heaven in a brutal war against all who defy His rightful reign. Revelation 19:19, 21 says, "And I saw the beast, the kings of the earth, and their armies, gathered together to make war against Him who sat on the horse and against His army. . . . And the rest were killed with the sword which proceeded from the mouth of Him who sat on the horse. And all the birds were filled with their flesh."

None of this is pretty, and none of this is exciting. But it's a reality, and war is with us.

But there's coming a time of peace.

A Kingdom of Peace

Someone has observed that in Washington, DC, there is a huge assortment of peace monuments. This is not because we value peace; it's because we build a new monument after every war. So we have a lot of peace monuments in Washington.

When you think back on the great leaders of history, you'll quickly make the connection that most of them became textbook-worthy because of their participation in war. Ancient rulers were masters of war, including Ramses, Cyrus, and Darius. Throughout history, we find that most of the people who did mighty things were people who were products of war. Napoleon, George Washington, Abraham Lincoln, and Winston Churchill—all of them used war as a tool to accomplish their aims.

There is one leader who did not. And that was Jesus. Once the Millennium is established, the kingdom of Christ will be on display, and it will be a kingdom of peace. The Bible says there won't be any more war. There will be peace.

Peace from God

First, there will be peace from God.

As we've seen, during that period of time, there will be an absentee member of the universe. And that person will be Satan. He will be locked away in the bottomless pit, and he won't have any influence on the wars. He won't be able to make war worse than it already is.

The psalmist describes the Lord as the One who "makes wars cease to the end of the earth; He breaks the bow and cuts the spear in two; He burns the chariot in the fire" (Psalm 46:9).

According to Scripture, when we get to the Golden Age, God will end every war. He doesn't end wars on just one or two continents. He stops them to the ends of the earth. Today there are wars or conflicts ongoing over the entire world—from Ukraine to Gaza to Yemen to Sudan to Myanmar to Ethiopia. And one day, the God of all peace will bring peace to all the world. He will break all the instruments of war and throw them into the fire. And war will be history.

Psalm 72 was written by King Solomon on the occasion of his coronation. This psalm was to be prayed by God's people on behalf of their king. Verse 7 says, "In His days the righteous shall flourish, and abundance of peace, until the moon is no more." During the coming Golden Age, peace will flourish.

The Millennium is the reverse of the curse. It's everything that God intended the world to be until man sinned. God will bring all of that back, and during the Millennium there will be a kind of perfection, though not total perfection. Peace will reign where war now reigns.

God is going to pour out an abundance of peace on all the nations. Isaiah described it this way: "The work of righteousness will be peace, and the effect of righteousness, quietness and assurance forever. My people will dwell in a peaceful habitation, in secure dwellings, and in quiet resting places" (32:17–18). The effect of the reign of Jesus will be quietness and peace.

Isaiah 54:13 says, "All your children shall be taught by the LORD, and great shall be the peace of your children." Great peace will be passed on to our children. What a joy that will be for everyone.

So there will be peace from God.

Peace Among Nations

There will also be peace among the nations. The prophet Micah was especially vivid in portraying the unprecedented peace of Jesus' rule. He says, "Now it shall come to pass in the latter days. . . . Many nations shall come and say, 'Come, and let us go up to the mountain of the LORD, to the house of the God of Jacob; He will teach us His ways, and we shall walk in His paths.' For out of Zion the law shall go forth, and the word of the LORD from Jerusalem" (4:1–2).

One commentator says, "The goal of [King Jesus'] teaching is the practical direction of people's lives so they will end up walking in ways consistent with God's ways. His powerful presence and persuasive message will transform the thinking and behavior of millions."[6]

Micah described the consequences of Jesus' reign. He wrote what has become one of the most famous prophecies about the Millennium in the Bible. Micah 4:3 says, "He shall judge between many peoples, and rebuke strong nations afar off; they shall beat their swords into plowshares, and their spears into pruning hooks; nation shall not lift up sword against nation, neither shall they learn war anymore."

In this powerful image, God sits as the ultimate judge of the world. He removes every reason for war; He rebukes those in the wrong. Weapons of destruction are melted down and repurposed for agricultural use. During the Millennium, life will be preserved and enhanced, not taken away and destroyed.

Notice that God won't bring about peace through force or coercion. Instead, each nation will renounce their desire to wage war against others.

Will there ever be worldwide peace during your lifetime and mine? No, there will not be. As soon as one problem is solved, somebody starts another one in another place that has implications for people in other places. And then war is back on again.

Does this mean we should stop trying for peace? No. But we shouldn't be disappointed when we don't get there, because there will never be peace on this earth until Jesus Christ comes back.

M. R. DeHaan wrote the following:

> The Bible is replete with prophecies of a coming age of peace and prosperity. It will be a time when war will be utterly unknown. Not a single armament plant will be operating, not a soldier or sailor will be in uniform, no military camps will exist, and not one cent will be spent for armaments of war, not a single penny will be used for defense, much less for offensive warfare. Can you imagine such an age, when all nations shall be at perfect peace, all the resources available for enjoyment, all industry engaged in the articles of a peaceful luxury?[7]

Is that possible? Not now. But there's coming a day when King Jesus, the Prince of Peace, will sit upon the throne of David and reign, and there will be true peace for a thousand years.

So will we ever know peace? If you are a Christian, you will ultimately get a chance to know peace on the earth during the Millennium.

Peace in Nature
And then there will be peace in nature.

Isaiah 55:12–13 says, "You shall go out with joy, and be led out with peace; the mountains and the hills shall break forth into singing before you, and all the trees of the field shall clap their hands. Instead of the thorn shall come up the cypress tree, and instead of the brier shall come up the myrtle tree; and it shall be to the LORD for a name, for an everlasting sign."

Are the mountains going to sing and the trees clap? No, that's a symbol given to us by the prophet to help us understand that when peace reigns on the earth, it cannot but help affect even nature. I don't expect to hear the mountains singing or see the trees clapping. But in that time of peace when Christ is on the throne, you're going to have a different feeling. You will know that you're in a land protected by the One who loves you dearly and died for you on the cross.

The transformation of the world following the lifting of the curse is observable. And this is a description of what's going to happen in the thousand-year reign of Christ.

One transformation is even taking place now. Isaiah 35:1–2 says, "The desert shall rejoice and blossom as the rose; it shall blossom abundantly and rejoice." There's a lot of desert in Israel. When you go to Israel, you normally stay near Galilee first. Then you go from Galilee down to Jerusalem, and you go through the desert. When I first started visiting Israel, all you saw in the desert were tents. Now, when you take that ride, you see that produce is in the desert. There are tents covering the plants that have grown there. The Jewish people have learned how to take the water from the ocean and desalinate it, and now it's used to irrigate their land. They have taken land that was a desert and, as the Scripture requires, they made it blossom like the rose.

The Bible says in Isaiah 41:18–19, "I will open rivers in desolate heights, and fountains in the midst of the valleys; I will make the wilderness a pool of water, and the dry land springs of water. I will plant in the wilderness the cedar and the acacia tree."

When the Bible talks about peace during the Millennium, it emphasizes green landscapes, lush gardens, and pools of water. What an atmosphere of peace that is.

Peace Throughout Israel

And then, there will be peace throughout Israel.

One of the Bible's central texts on the coming Golden Age is found in Isaiah 60. Verse 18 says, "Violence shall no longer be heard in your land, neither wasting nor destruction within your borders; but you shall call your walls Salvation, and your gates Praise."

For a land that has known so much violence and destruction in its history, what a relief this must bring. In the coming kingdom of the

Messiah, bullying, assault, abuse, neglect, and murder will be unheard of within the borders of Israel. And not only that, but there will also be a lot of singing in Israel.

In that day, you will enter Zion with a song of praise. The Bible says when we get to the Millennium, we're going to sing a lot because we'll be at peace. We'll be filled with the joy of the Lord everywhere we go.

The Bible also says that when the Lord comes and His feet touch the Mount of Olives, the whole land of Israel is going to change. A mountain will come into Israel that will be the tallest mountain in the world. On top of this mountain will be Ezekiel's millennial temple that will be built on ten square miles, and the Bible says we will go up the Highway of Holiness to see God. We will have access to the throne of God, through Jesus Christ and Prince David. And what a joy that will be.

Isaiah 66:12 says, "Thus says the LORD: 'Behold, I will extend peace to [Israel] like a river.'" Peace like a river will flow into Israel.

Peace Between Enemies

This peace that Christ brings to the Millennium is going to destroy enmity between nations. Isaiah 19:23–25 says, "In that day there will be a highway from Egypt to Assyria, and the Assyrian will come into Egypt and the Egyptian into Assyria, and the Egyptians will serve with the Assyrians. In that day Israel will be one of three with Egypt and Assyria—a blessing in the midst of the land, whom the LORD of hosts shall bless, saying, 'Blessed is Egypt My people, and Assyria the work of My hands, and Israel My inheritance.'"

The Bible talks about these three former enemies going up the highway together, joined together in doing the work that needs to be done. God's Word, which is divine truth and cannot be deceiving, tells us this.

W. A. Criswell says about this particular verse:

Can you imagine a thing like that? Think of the bitterness among the Palestinian people. Think of the years of hatred ever since Ishmael and Isaac grew to despise one another. From that day until this has there ever not been war between Israel and the Arabs? But there is coming a time, says the Lord, when the Lord of hosts will bless them all, saying, "Blessed be Egypt my people, and blessed be Assyria the work of my hands, and blessed be Israel mine inheritance." All of us, saved Jews, and saved Gentiles, are to be together in the glorious and ultimate kingdom of our Lord.[8]

There will be no more enmity between these nations, and we shall study war no more. The Scripture says that there will be peace.

There's a man by the name of Hollis Godfrey who wrote an old science fiction novel called *The Man Who Ended War*. He published this in 1908, and the story follows a scientist who discovers a type of radiation that can dissolve metal in moments. As the only person possessing that technology, this scientist demands that the whole world unilaterally disarm and dismantle all their weapons of war.

Of course, it's all fiction. The scientist has no power to do that, even if he has some special invention. But it points to one thing—there is coming a Man who can do that. And that Man is our Savior, our King, the Lord Jesus Christ. He is the Man who will end all war. We will dissolve all our implements of warfare into implements of agriculture, and for one thousand years we will live on the earth in peace with one another. No uprisings, no war.

There's another kind of war that most are quite aware of. Not the war in the world; it's the war that goes on in our hearts. The Bible says that there are two energies going on in our hearts. There's the enemy called Satan who wants to take us into his kingdom, and there's Jesus Christ who wants us to come be with Him. God created you with a space in your heart that belongs to God alone. Until you allow Him to have that space and occupy it, you will always be at war. But you can make peace with God, and that war can be over.

You can also have war going on in your heart as a Christian because you've got the old nature and the new nature. Paul said in Romans 7:19, "For the good that I will to do, I do not do; but the evil I will not to do, that I practice." Until we place Jesus Christ on the throne of our hearts, we will always be at war with God. Is Jesus Christ now on the throne of your life? Or are you running the show? Put Jesus Christ in control and watch what He does to bring peace to you in your heart right now. You don't have to wait for peace of heart until the Millennium. You can have it today if you put Christ, the Prince of Peace, on the throne of your life.

APPLICATION

Personal Questions

1. What are your thoughts on war?

2. The Bible has a lot to say about war, particularly in the Old Testament.

    a. What command did God give Moses in Deuteronomy 3:2–4?

    b. According to Joshua 15:63 and 17:13, what did the Israelites fail to do after entering the promised land?

3. Read Revelation 19:19–21. What do these verses tell us about the moment when Christ comes back at the end of the Tribulation?

4. How does Psalm 46:9 describe the Lord?

5. Read Psalm 72:7. How is the Millennium described in this verse?

6. Read Micah 4:1–3.

   a. What will the nations do during the coming Golden Age according to verses 1–2?

   b. What will happen to weapons of war during this time (see verse 3)?

7. Read Isaiah 41:18–19 and 55:12–13. What do these verses teach us about peace in nature during the Millennium?

8. Describe the peace that will exist in Israel during the thousand-year reign of Christ.

9. Read Romans 7:13–25.

   a. What war did Paul mention in these verses?

b. Describe a time you experienced this war in your own heart. How did you find peace in that moment?

Group Questions

1. Discuss how war has impacted our world throughout history and how it is still impacting it today.

2. Read James 4:1–2 together.

   a. What is the real reason for wars according to these verses?

   b. Discuss how these verses relate to current wars or ones in recent history.

3. Read Joshua 15:63 and 17:13 as a group.

   a. What did the Israelites do to the Canaanites instead of following God's command to drive them from the land?

b. What were the future consequences of their disobedience?

4. Read Psalm 46:9 and 72:7 together. What do these two verses tell us about the role of war in the coming Golden Age?

5. Read the following verses from Isaiah and describe the peace each verse mentions.

a. Isaiah 32:17–18

b. Isaiah 54:13

c. Isaiah 55:12–13

d. Isaiah 35:1–2

e. Isaiah 41:18–19

f. Isaiah 60:18

g. Isaiah 66:12

h. Isaiah 19:23–25

6. As a group, read Romans 7:13–25 and discuss the war that Paul felt within himself.

    a. What are some strategies for winning the war within our heart?

    b. What are some practical ways you can encourage each other to continue to say no to sin?

DID YOU KNOW?

If you visit the gardens of the United Nations in New York City, you might see the bronze sculpture by Soviet artist Evgeniy Vuchetich depicting a man holding a hammer aloft in one hand and beating a sword into a plow. It's called *Let Us Beat Swords Into Ploughshares*. The sculpture suggests that one of the missions of the United Nations is converting implements of war into implements of peace and productivity. Of course, the United Nations has utterly failed in that mission. All human efforts for true, lasting peace will not come to fruition until Christ returns to set up His kingdom.

Notes
1. Vladimir Isachenkov, Dasha Litvinova, Yuras Karmanau, and Jim Heintz, "Russia Attacks Ukraine as Defiant Putin Warns US, NATO," *Associated Press*, February 23, 2022, https://apnews.com/article/russia-ukraine-europe-russia-moscow-kyiv-626a8c5ec22217bacb24ece60fac4fe1.
2. Helene Cooper, Thomas Gibbons-Neff, Eric Schmitt, and Julian E. Barnes, "Troop Deaths and Injuries in Ukraine War Near 500,000, U.S. Officials Say," *New York Times*, August 18, 2023, https://www.nytimes.com/2023/08/18/us/politics/ukraine-russia-war-casualties.html.
3. "Ukraine Emergency," *UNHCR*, accessed March 26, 2024, https://www.unrefugees.org/emergencies/ukraine/.
4. Chris Hedges, "What Every Person Should Know About War," *New York Times*, July 6, 2003, https://www.nytimes.com/2003/07/06/books/chapters/what-every-person-should-know-about-war.html.
5. C. S. Lewis, "Reflections: Truths Ancient and Simple," *C. S. Lewis Institute*, June 1, 2017, https://www.cslewisinstitute.org/resources/reflections-june-2017/.
6. Gary V. Smith, *The NIV Application Commentary: Hosea, Amos, Micah* (Grand Rapids, MI: Zondervan, 2001), 508.
7. M. R. DeHaan, *The Great Society* (Radio Bible Class, 1965), 7–8.
8. W. A. Criswell, *Expository Sermons on Revelation, Volume 5* (Grand Rapids, MI: Zondervan, 1966), 790.

LEADER'S GUIDE

Thank you for your commitment to lead a group through *The Coming Golden Age*. Being a leader has its own rewards. You may discover that your walk with the Lord deepens through this experience. Throughout the study guide, your group will explore new topics and review study questions that encourage thought-provoking group discussion.

The lessons in this study guide are suitable for Sunday school classes, small-group studies, elective Bible studies, or home Bible study groups. Each lesson is structured to provoke thought and help you grow in your knowledge and understanding of God. There are multiple components in this section that can help you structure your lessons and discussion time, so make sure you read and consider each one.

Before You Begin

Before you begin each meeting, make sure you and your group are well-versed with the content of the lesson. Group members should have their own study guide so they can follow along and write in the study guide if need be. You may wish to assign the study guide lesson as homework prior to the meeting of the group and then use the meeting time to discuss the lesson.

To ensure that everyone has a chance to participate in the discussion, the ideal size for a group is around eight to ten people. If there are more than ten people, try to break up the bigger group into smaller subgroups. Make sure the members are committed to participating each week, as this will help create stability and help you better prepare the structure of the meeting.

At the beginning of the study each week, start the session with a question to challenge group members to think about the issues you will be discussing. The members can answer briefly, but the goal is to have an idea in their mind as you go over the lesson. This allows the group members to become engaged and ready to interact with the group.

After reviewing the lesson, try to initiate a free-flowing discussion. Invite group members to bring questions and insights they may have discovered to the next meeting, especially if they were unsure of the meaning of some parts of the lesson. Be prepared to discuss how biblical truth applies to the world we live in today.

Weekly Preparation

As the group leader, here are a few things that you can do to prepare for each meeting:

- *Make sure you are thoroughly familiar with the material in the lesson.* Make sure that you understand the content of the lesson so you know how to structure the group time and are prepared to lead group discussion.

- *Decide, ahead of time, which questions you want to discuss.* Depending on how much time you have each week, you may not be able to reflect on every question. Select specific questions that you feel will evoke the best discussion.

- *Take prayer requests.* At the end of your discussion, take prayer requests from your group members and pray for each other.

Structuring the Discussion Time

As the group leader, it is up to you to keep track of the time and keep things moving along according to your schedule. If your group is having a good discussion, don't feel the need to stop and move on to the next question. Remember, the purpose is to pull together ideas and share unique insights on the lesson. Make time each week to discuss how to apply these truths to living for Christ today.

The purpose of discussion is for everyone to participate, but don't be concerned if certain group members are more quiet—they may be internally reflecting on the questions and need time to process their ideas before they can share them.

If you need help in organizing your time when planning your group Bible study, the following schedule, for sixty minutes and ninety minutes, can give you a structure for the lesson:

Section	60 Minutes	90 Minutes
WELCOME: Members arrive and get settled	5 minutes	10 minutes
GETTING STARTED QUESTION: Prepares the group for interacting with one another	10 minutes	10 minutes
MESSAGE: Review the lesson	15 minutes	25 minutes
DISCUSSION: Discuss group study questions	25 minutes	35 minutes
PRAYER AND APPLICATION : Final application for the week and prayer before dismissal	5 minutes	10 minutes

Group Dynamics

Leading a group study can be a rewarding experience for you and your group members—but that doesn't mean there won't be challenges. Certain members may feel uncomfortable discussing topics that they consider very personal and might be afraid of being called on. Some members might have disagreements on specific issues. To help prevent these scenarios, consider the following ground rules:

- If someone has a question that may seem off topic, suggest that it is discussed at another time, or ask the group if they are okay with addressing that topic.

- If someone asks a question you don't know the answer to, confess that you don't know and move on. If you feel comfortable, invite other group members to give their opinions or share their comments based on personal experience.

• If you feel like a couple of people are talking much more than others, direct questions to people who may not have shared yet. You could even ask the more dominating members to help draw out the quiet ones.

• When there is a disagreement, encourage the group members to process the matter in love. Invite members from opposing sides to evaluate their opinions and consider the ideas of the other members. Lead the group through Scripture that addresses the topic, and look for common ground.

When issues arise, encourage your group to think of Scripture: "Love one another" (John 13:34), "If it is possible, as far as it depends on you, live at peace with everyone" (Romans 12:18 NIV), and "Be quick to listen, slow to speak and slow to become angry" (James 1:19 NIV).

DR. DAVID JEREMIAH
AND TURNING POINT

D r. David Jeremiah is the founder of Turning Point, a ministry committed to providing Christians with sound Bible teaching relevant to today's changing times through radio and television broadcasts, audio series, books, and live events. Dr. Jeremiah's common-sense teaching on topics such as family, prayer, worship, angels, and biblical prophecy forms the foundation of Turning Point.

David and his wife, Donna, reside in El Cajon, California, where he serves as the senior pastor of Shadow Mountain Community Church. They have four children, twelve grandchildren, and one great-grandchild.

In 1982, Dr. Jeremiah brought the same solid teaching to San Diego television that he shares weekly with his congregation. Shortly thereafter, Turning Point expanded its ministry to radio. Dr. Jeremiah's inspiring messages can now be heard worldwide on radio, television, and the Internet.

Because Dr. Jeremiah desires to know his listening audience, he travels nationwide holding ministry events that touch the hearts and lives of many people. According to Dr. Jeremiah, "At some point in time, everyone reaches a turning point; and for every person, that moment is unique, an experience to hold onto forever. There's so much changing in today's world that sometimes it's difficult to choose the right path. Turning Point offers people an understanding of God's Word as well as the opportunity to make a difference in their lives."

Dr. David Jeremiah has authored numerous books, including *Escape the Coming Night* (Revelation), *The Handwriting on the Wall* (Daniel), *Prayer—The Great Adventure*, *Agents of the Apocalypse*, *Agents of Babylon*, *A Life Beyond Amazing*, *Overcomer*, *Everything You Need*, *Forward*, *The Jesus You May Not Know*, *The God You May Not Know*, *Where Do We Go From Here?*, *The World of the End*, and *The Great Disappearance*.

stay connected to the teaching of

DR. DAVID JEREMIAH

· · · · · · · ·

Publishing | Radio | Television | Online

FURTHER YOUR STUDY OF THE BOOK

· · · · · · · ·

The Coming Golden Age Resource Materials

To enhance your study on this important topic, we recommend the correlating audio message album and DVD messages from the *The Coming Golden Age* series with Dr. David Jeremiah.

Audio Message Album

The material found in this book originated from messages presented by Dr. Jeremiah at Shadow Mountain Community Church where he serves as senior pastor. These messages are conveniently packaged in an accessible audio album.

DVD Message Presentations

Watch Dr. Jeremiah deliver the *The Coming Golden Age* original messages in this special DVD collection.

To order these products, call us at 1-800-947-1993 or visit us online at www.DavidJeremiah.org.

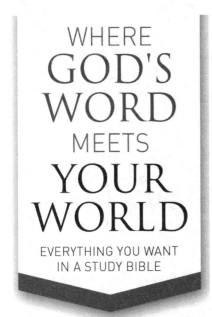
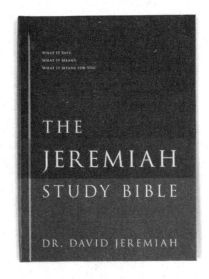

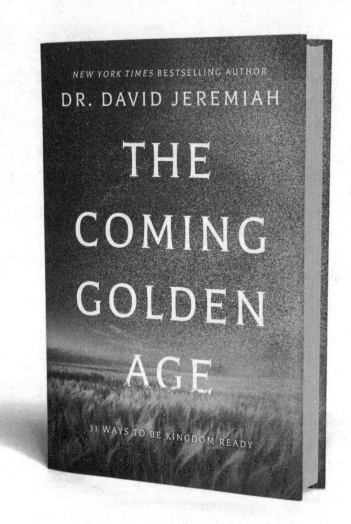